CHAK
MEDITATION
FOR BEGINNERS

COMPLETE GUIDE TO CHAKRAS
MEDITATION PRACTICES FOR AURA
CLEANSING, ENERGY RECOVERY AND
BALANCE OF EMOTIONS TO IMPROVE
RELATIONSHIPS.

Judy Keys

TABLE OF CONTENTS

Introduction

Meditation, at its most basic level, is the practice of concentrating the mind on a particular thing. All forms of meditation that are common today are rooted in a specific spiritual tradition and have been developed to focus the mind on the divine. Many advanced meditation practices of those cultures have been kept secret (though they can now be found throughout the internet). They were only available to nuns, monks, priests, and other followers who gave everything up to learn these secret techniques and gain clarity.

By renouncing all worldly activities and submitting to a master, guru, or church's discipline, among them specific methods of meditation and respiration, a person demonstrated his important trust in such secret lessons, designed to bring a person into a distorted state of consciousness. Ultimately, if a student was faithful in his or her spiritual teacher or church's guidance and lessons, he/she could achieve a state known as a divine union. However, while the names are different, the experience of religious unity is always the same for those who make it. The state of divine unity is called many different things as satori, nirvana, or the kingdom of heaven. The practitioner who enters religious union experiences expanded consciousness where he/she feels immersed in another world, of which he/she is a member, but also totally beyond.

The fact that all meditation techniques are rooted in a particular religious' tradition cannot be ignored. If you are an atheist, it will be difficult to find practices that do not point to anything beyond that at some level as the source of all life. Even if you're not an atheist, before starting your meditation, you have to deal with this reality. Otherwise, you will be confused and frustrated. Some Westerners, for example, can easily incorporate Eastern meditation into their lives. Eastern traditions, however, rely on specific concepts, such as karma and reincarnation. In some cultures, Eastern meditation also requires total separation from all worldly pursuits.

From a western perspective, meditation means thinking deeply and carefully about something. It also means focusing on a subject. It typically has religious connotations. Reflections, which are concentrated or profound, are usually done on spiritual things.

We also use "meditate" to relax and talk about something in our everyday language.

Meditation means something very different from an eastern point of view. And understanding is not very easy. Essentially, it means something like a frame of a picture. But we can hardly say that.

Various people have different concepts of what is eastern meditation. Due to the current recent awareness about meditation, people may have a different conception of what meditation is. It may be extraordinarily esoteric and tough to understand if we try to think of meditation directly concerning its real essence. This can prevent people from trying to understand more about it.

The best way to learn more about meditation, start with some basic notions related to meditation, and slowly gain an understanding of meditation.

We all know about physical training. We exercise to develop our muscles, to ton them, and to acquire physical strength. We know that we can use physically and train body parts (muscles) and increase physical fitness.

Like the physical exercise of the muscles, I want to say that we have to train our minds to improve our mental health. You may not agree, so support me. You may not agree. We will expand on what I mean gradually through terms such as "train the mind" and "mental well-being."

We know we don't need to train all our organs necessarily. Our lungs, kidneys, liver, etc. must not be prepared. Many parts and bodies of our bodies need no specialized training or attention. They perform their tasks without any particular notice.

We usually believe that our mind requires no special attention. But we're right. I ask you to re-examine this conviction. When we speak more about meditation, we understand precisely why mind learning is essential.

We loosely know that it is imperative to be able to pay attention to. You must have seen that in a classroom when the teacher explained something critical, you lost concentration and began to think about something else in your mind. To know later that an essential point that the instructor addressed was overlooked.

You have just missed the critical discussion and the crucial point. You either had to learn about that or go and tell the teacher more. You could quickly compensate for that inattention, of course. But wouldn't it be useful if you had less of these incidents?

Such deficiencies occur much more than you realize. We miss essential discussions not only in classrooms but at workplace meetings. You would probably miss the job your partner wanted you to do as you thought about something else when he or she let you know what had to be done.

Think about it. Think about it. If we can not focus our attention on the task at hand, we could easily get distracted. We know that distractions make us inefficient and fall short of our deadlines.

If you are driving a car or are a tightrope walker, you may be killed by a lack of focused attention!

It is human nature. It is human nature. We can't always have perfect focus or attention. But the key is that we can easily benefit from focusing on the subject at hand. The sharper and better focus is part of the psychological well-being we mentioned above.

Put, meditation is about improving our focus or attention. It's about better concentration. Sound straightforward, right? Yes, meditation is training the mind to enhance strength or awareness. That is undoubtedly the starting point to understand the meditation correctly.

You can see that your attention is improved immediately. The default character of our mind is that if we find an activity that is very interesting to us, our brain can easily focus on the movement without delay. We should keep focusing on the task without distracting ourselves from other issues.

But if the activity isn't so enjoyable for us, it's elementary for us to miss out on things other than the event.

The state of mind also depends on our attention. I mean that we are concerned with some disturbing events or possibilities of worrying developments; such concern can easily distract us from the activity. The care must not be adverse; a fear for positive events such as anticipation of a happy or enjoyable activity may also distract you quickly from the current task.

Chapter 1 Chakras and Science

For a long time, science was unable, or unwilling, to explore the chakras and chakra healing. While there is still limited Western science "backing up" the chakra energy centers, it is clear that your body functions thanks to the systems or energetic impulses inside it. Everything you do and think is controlled by this system of energy, which Western science has proven time and time again. Simply looking at the brain's electrical pulses shows how energy rules this vital organ. Before modern science, the chakras were a good method for describing how the body functioned or was even able to function. Now, science may have labeled these properties something different or still cannot explain why certain things in your body works the way they do, but there are some things that this ancient science and today's modern understanding do agree on.

The first thing that science and the charkas agree on is that your body is made up of energy, and so is everything else around you. In fact, nothing around you is actually a solid piece of reality; it is simply a collection of energy particles deciding to hold together for a short time. Think about a chair. It may appear solid and sturdy to you; however, at its most basic level, it is just a combination of atoms. Atoms are not solid or static items. Inside these atoms are even smaller particles that are constantly moving and adjusting. Those particles are not solid, either. These particles inside the atom are called subatomic particles and are the electrons, neutrons, and protons. The neutrons and protons huddle together at the center of the atom, while the electrons race around on the outside. These move so quickly that scientists cannot determine where an electron is exactly at from one instance to the next.

In addition to being made up of energy and racing electrons and huddling subatomic particles, an atom is mostly made up of space. In fact, it is estimated that each atom is 99.99% space. This space is what allows for all this movement. And this information is true, not just about your chair, but about everything around you and you yourself! Your body and mind are always moving and changing, much more subtle than you may ever feel or know. Nothing in this world exists without energy.

Science now is able to understand and prove this, but religions have understood for thousands of years the powerful role energy plays in your life. Chakras, tai chi, yoga, QiGong, and reiki are all examples of spiritual practices that deal with moving your energy. And the purpose of this movement is to help your body and your existence find a state of well-being and harmony. These ancient religions understand that we are influenced by and can similarly influence back, this transference and movement of energy through your actions, including your thoughts. This is because your brain is also moving and thoughts are your reality.

Science has begun to explain some of this movement and

transference. For example, even when you are sleeping, your body is moving energy around. According to science, this happens mainly through your neurons and nerve pathways. In the ancient sciences and spirituality, it was explained through the chakras and the nadis. No matter what you are consciously or unconsciously doing, your body is a course of flowing energy. This includes digesting your food, thinking, moving your limbs, breathing, and even healing yourself.

The signals the nervous system transmits go from the brain to the body and from the body back to the brain. There are receptors all along the length of your body and all throughout, so you can coordinate your actions with your needs and wants. Again, this includes both the conscious and unconscious actions your body takes. When you lift your arm, you are making use of your nervous system and sending energy to your arm to lift it up. When you eat something, your body begins a series of energetic processes to digest, absorb, and remove the waste of that food. These are examples of voluntary and involuntary actions that require energy and communication between receptors and your brain.

In ancient religions, there are many ways to move this energy so it can continue to support the proper functioning of your body. Things like yoga poses, meditation, and breathing practices are all ways to move energy and restore harmonious balance in your life. Chakra healing and balancing is another method, and this often includes a combination of various techniques to move your energy. Both quantum mechanics and "traditional" science suggest that focusing on your thoughts can make a large difference in your overall well-being. For example, visualization techniques have been successfully used to help improve mental functioning and prevent deterioration of the brain in patients that suffered negative side effects from a stroke. Focusing on the chakras and the movement of energy through the nadis is a great method, used for thousands of years and supported through modern science, for bringing peace and well-being to your life. It may be called something different, but it is really similar to one another.

Your energetic body, made up of these subtle energetic impulses, is best revealed in your heart and brain. Your brain is probably one of the best places to "look" to see how powerful energy is at work in your body. In your brain alone, there are more than one hundred billion "wires" that conduct energetic impulses. These impulses are actually charged up ions coursing through your body, making sure your heart is pumping and your muscles are moving. They are biological pathways that are critical to your proper functioning. Observing the electricity of the brain is a great way to understand how your body is made up of energy.

In addition to the energy living inside of you, there is energy surrounding your body, too. It is often hard to comprehend when you see and feel the boundary of skin and know the solidity of bones, but there is an electromagnetic field surrounding your body. This has a certain frequency. This can seem like New Age and ancient "non-sense" until you realize that scientist uses this understanding when they measure these frequencies with machines like an MRI or ECG machine. A change in energy in a certain location tells them something is out of balance, and they can see it through the image these machines produce.

Psychology is another modern scientific field that examines the mind and why we think and behave in certain ways. According to Psychology Today, every person is a physical embodiment of an energetic field. The chakras go further to explain that there are centers in the body for this energy to flow through. These movements control your emotions, organs, and immune system, among other things. When all things are flowing as they should, you are balanced spiritually, physically, emotionally, and mentally. That is why your chakras are so important to your overall well-being.

On the contrary, if there is a blockage in your energy, you become ill. This is seen in scientific tests such as a CT scan or an MRI. A tumor appears like a black spot in an otherwise energetic and moving system. It is blocking your energy in that place and you are not well. Other times, it manifests in your mental ability. An energy block can cause mental illness such as anxiety, depression, or more. Practicing ways to clear and move your energy is a powerful tool. A recent study showed that participants that suffered from a stroke saw marked improvements in the health of their brain when they spent time visualizing lifting a limb that was paralyzed during the stroke. The stroke damaged a part of their brain that sends the energetic information to that limb to move but visualizing it moving helped strengthen the brain tissue around that damaged area so the deterioration did not spread. This is just one modern scientific example of how an ancient tradition of moving energy with your thoughts can cause significant improvement to your physical well-being.

Your mental state is known to impact your physical body. We see this most in the correlation between stress and your health. Stress is an emotional and mental state, but when it is too prevalent, it causes a cascade of physical ailments along with it. According to the National Institute of Health, stress is an imbalance in your life. This imbalance, real or perceived, triggers the body to try to find and restore balance. These situations cause stress release hormones that are incredibly powerful and that lead to the feeling of anxiety and stimulation. Contemporary science lists stress as a major factor in numerous illnesses, such as cancer and mental illness. Stress costs millions of dollars a year in medical expenses. This is a constant discussion in modern science and most doctors and scientists agree that reducing stress is vital in supporting your overall health.

In addition, contemporary science and medicine are beginning to understand and promote healthy mental health alongside physical health. It has become more and more obvious that a person's mental state is as important, if not more so, than their physical body in restoring balance in their overall health. Good treatment not only includes treating the physical body but the mental and spiritual as well. According to the National Institute of Health, most books dealing with the spiritual or mental treatment of an individual is more spiritual in nature, keeping the topic foreign to most physicians, but Western medicine must begin to create a more comprehensive model to treat the gross and subtle bodies of a person. This means Western science needs to continue their understanding of how the energy in the mind and spirit connect to the physical body as they treat patients.

Almost a century ago, in the West, Sir William Osler documented a case where a patient suffered from an asthma attack after smelling an artificial rose. This posed a curious question that science, at the time, could not explain. There was no physical reason that this should have happened. Dr. Robert Adler, in 1975, offered an explanation to this question; a person's thoughts can control their immune system. Sir William Osler was curious about why mammals were able to have controlled immune responses, and Dr. Adler was finally able to explain it. In his experiments, Dr. Adler was able to prove that a person's emotions and thoughts could create significant changes in their physical body and immune system.

Before these findings, Western science thought each body system worked independently of one another. The foundation of our modern science considered your immune system to not be impacted by your emotional or mental state. Dr. Adler proved this is not the case. His findings showed that, indeed, your entire body works together impacting each part to find balance or homeostasis. It was also his findings that first explained that stress negatively impacts your physical well-being.

You can finally begin to see more traditional, Western doctors embracing the understanding that your mental state is a major impact on your physical body, but it is something that Eastern traditions have known for thousands of years. Ancient science knew that energy is life and an imbalance in this energy, in any form, disrupts your physical existence. Energy needs to flow freely, and one of the best ways you can do this is by taking certain actions to find this balance. You can use meditation, visualization, eating certain foods, performing certain physical actions, etc. to move this life force, or vital energy, through your body and find balance. When you can keep these hubs or channels of energy clear, like keeping plaque out of your arteries for proper blood flow, you can live a more healthy and harmonious life. Unfortunately, many Western cultures do not focus on this integrated approach. This results in dormant, inactive, or blocked energy centers. This leads to a disruption in the flow of energy, and ultimately, to disease and imbalance.

Living With Your Own Energy

Once you have accepted the power of your journey of self-discovery, you can begin to live your life every day with this understanding and connection to your chakras. We all have jobs, rent, bills, obligations, relationships, activities, and all manner of things that need taking care of in our lives. There are no rules for how you choose to live or how you incorporate your healing practices into your daily life; only you know the true answers to that. There are several things that can help you stay aligned in your chakras, however, that can be a great way for you to get started with empowering your journey.

As you begin to shift and heal your chakras, take into consideration how you are currently living your life. Some of those ways are:

- Excessive drugs, substances, alcohol

- Poor diet

- Lack of exercise

- Abusive or manipulative relationships

- Excessive television viewing, screen time, social media

- Dead end jobs that cause anxiety, depression, and stress
- Family issues

There are so many more ways that your chakras can collect energy that keeps you blocked and cloudy and in order to heal well, you

19

will need to make some serious lifestyle changes. Before you get overly concerned about how that must occur, pay attention to why you are feeling that way in the first place. You may be excited to turn your life upside down and give yourself a new adventure toward the life you want. If you feel scared, worried, uncomfortable, skeptical or resistant to making any of the changes in lifestyle mentioned above, then you are in need of some serious energy clearing in some or all of your chakras.

The point of healing your energy is to help you align with your true purpose as a person in your life. How can you live your whole truth if you are unwell, unhappy, energetically imbalanced and suffering from significant blocks in your system?

Making the choice to clear your chakras is a big enough step in itself. No matter how long it takes you, even if it takes years, if you are committed to healing your chakras, then you will find the life you are looking for. Here are some of the ways you can promote life changes to help you heal and live with your own energy as your guide:

Make time to meditate everyday to improve your journey and open yourself more quickly.

- Choose yourself first, before you choose others.

- Ask yourself how you are feeling whenever it feels right to do so. Keep a healthy, open communication with yourself, your feelings and your energy.

- Learn more about how you can open your chakras through yoga, breathing exercises, crystal therapies, acupuncture, massage therapy, Reiki and more.

- Take time in nature. Schedule time when you can be alone in the woods or on a hike.

- Practice oneness with yourself by being alone and tuning into your energy multiple times a day. Chakra check ins can be an excellent way to stay involved with your energy shifts.

- Take some new classes to awaken your chakras. You may find a ballet or dance class for your sacral chakra, or a painting class. You might find a writing class to open your throat chakra. You can take a class in pottery to connect you to your root and the earth. You could also start getting an education in the vocation you have always wanted to pursue but were too afraid to which will open and purge all of your chakras on some level.

- Bond with your personal space and make sure it feels right for your healing journey.

- Open up to loved ones about your experiences and let love in while you do so.

- Move to a new apartment or house in a neighborhood that feels safer or more affordable for your lifestyle needs.

- Change your job to something more like who you are, not what you think you have to be.

- Engage in healthier relationships and be willing to say goodbye to the ones that keep you stuck and away from healing yourself.

- Bravely accept that your energy is always with you and a part of your life and is affected by everything you do, experience, choose and think.

All of these offerings are meant as guidance and support; a creative way for you to get started living with your own energy. Take your time moving forward. You don't have to change all at once. You will find that it happens naturally and slowly with your chakra healing experience and you won't have to think about it all that mush. Living with and accepting your energy offers it a chance to guide you. It is who you truly are and when you are cleansed, clear, purged, and unblocked in your chakras, your life can flow more freely and smoothly.

Living with your energy is a life practice and you are the one who will decide how to make all of the changes you need to make to have a healthy energetic life. Your chakras are ready for you to make the right decisions for you and will guide you forward, no matter what. Listen to your chakras and learn to live with your own energy.

Chapter 2 The seven Chakras

The chakras are the centers of energy inside of the body that influences the spiritual, emotional, mental, and physical well-being of a person. Each individual chakra will have its own name, color, and characteristics and will control a different area of the body. Modern interest in the ancient world of chakras grew during the peace and love-filled the 1960s when hippies were looking for new ways to achieve balance in the world.

There are seven levels of chakras and they do correspond with the different systems of the body. The chakras work together to give overall balance to the body. These centers of energy do contain and process all of the energy in the body. The chakras hold the power to sustain human life or destroy it. As the keeper of the energy, they can drive you, but when they become unbalanced or blocked they can prevent your progress or even send your health on a downward spiral.

Each one of the chakras has a special color which is linked to the aura they produce. The intensity of the color can easily change. In a healthy person, the colors will be beautifully bright and clear. But if the person is not feeling well, when they are angry, or when there is stress present in the person's life, the colors of the aura will fade as the chakras begin to lose control over the body. If someone is physically or emotionally impaired the chakras might completely lose their color. If a chakra is closed or blocked, then the energy contained within it can be stagnant or slow and that will affect the organs and the body parts which that chakra is attached to. But if a chakra has an abundance of energy it will absorb the energy stored in nearby chakras and it can overwhelm the energy system entirely.

Every chakra has a correspondence with one of the natural elements of fire, water, air, earth and the spiritual element that is known as ether. And every chakra has a theme that is associated with one particular part of life and living.

Each chakra has its own color that is associated with its particular energy. The colors of the chakras follow the colors of the rainbow. They are a visual demonstration of the entire color spectrum. Rainbows and chakras contain all of the colors that humans are able to see. Don't think of the colors individually but rather as a spectrum that begins at the bottom at the spine and continues upward through the top of the head. Just as the colors in the rainbow blend together and complement each other, so do the individual chakras work together while standing alone.

The First Chakra: The Root Chakra

The path through the system of chakras begins with the root chakra. This is the very center of a human's primal needs, security, and the center of survival. The color selected for the Root Chakra is red and its element is earth. Found at the very bottom of the spine, the Root Chakra is associated with the bowels, feet, and legs. Its theme is 'to be'. The chakra uses for balance is the Crown chakra.

The color that represents the Root Chakra is red, which is a completely physical color. Red promotes a feeling of being connected to the earth and of being grounded. The color makes people think of feelings and thoughts of instinct and survival. Red usually makes a person feel primal, vigilant, and alert.

This chakra is considered to be the very foundation of the entire system of energy. It is also the chakra that stores all of the excess energy for the other chakras. An excessive Root Chakra or one that is blocked or closed will give off definite symptoms:

- Nervousness

- Possessiveness and greed

- Irrational fears

- Excessive concerns regarding personal safety

- Financial problems

- A feeling of being loose or ungrounded

- Weakness in the knees or ankles

- Digestive issues such as IBS

The Root Chakra is overwhelmingly thought to be the foundation for all of the other chakras. Since it is associated with the bottom three vertebrae, the pelvic floor, and the end of the spine, the Root

Chakra is considered to be the foundation of the human body. This chakra is the one responsible for an individual's survival and sense of security. It is also connected to the need to be grounded in every way possible. Humans have basic needs for safety, shelter, food, and water. They also need to feel safe and are afraid to let go sometimes. These emotions are all grounded in the Root Chakra, and when it is balanced there comes a natural feeling of safety and security. A blocked Root Chakra can cause a wide variety of illnesses, both mental and physical. Mental ailments include nightmares, irrational fears, and anxiety disorders. The physical problems might include problems with the legs, feet, lower back, bladder, or colon.

The Second Chakra: The Sacral Chakra

This second chakra holds the key to a person's deepest sensations and emotions and controls how they are expressed and held within the body. This chakra also controls a person's potential creativity as well as the balance of yin and yang and of dark and light. The Sacral Chakra is deep within the lower part of the abdomen, under the belly button. Its color is orange and its element is water. The theme of the Sacral Chakra is 'to feel' and it corresponds to the lower back, hips, bladder, kidneys, and the reproductive system. Its balancing chakra is the Throat Chakra. If the Sacral Chakra becomes excessive or is blocked or closed it might give off the following symptoms:

- Shame or confusion over sexual matters

- Guilty feelings

- Kidney malfunctions or diseases

- Disorders of the reproductive system

- Bladder issues

- Emotional imbalances

- Various addictions

The Sacral Chakra is the one that is responsible for creativity and sexuality. People who have a well-balanced Sacral Chakra are fulfilled, passionate, and friendly. They give off feelings of joy, pleasure, abundance, and wellness. The key to keeping the Sacral Chakra working correctly is to feel free to express personal creativity and by honoring the body. A blocked Sacral Chakra will cause a person to feel emotionally unstable or creatively uninspired. It can also cause addictive behaviors, depression, and an overwhelming fear of change.

The Sacral Chakra is orange because orange is the color of energy and creativity. It gives people a sense of security and warmth. The color makes people think of feelings and thoughts of sexuality, pleasure, and passion. The color orange makes people feel abundant, safe, and sensual.

The key to enjoying a healthy Sacral Chakra is to maintain personal equilibrium while allowing creativity, pleasures, and emotions to flow freely. People who are overcome by emotions and desires can easily become distressed. The Sacral Chakra is strengthened by practices that encourage a deep emotional connection with other people and practicing the healthy, honest expression of one's self.

The Third Chakra: The Solar Plexus Chakra

Just above the belly button, inside of the upper abdomen, is the Solar Plexus Chakra. In this chakra is where a person's inner fire begins and grows to ignite willpower and self-confidence. Yellow is the color that was chosen for the Solar Plexus Chakra, and its element is fire. Its theme is 'to do' and it corresponds with the pancreas, liver, gallbladder, spleen, and the stomach. The Third Eye Chakra is the balancing chakra for the Solar Plexus Chakra. If a Solar Plexus Chakra is overly active or is closed or blocked, it may exhibit the following symptoms:

- Excessive anger

- Problems with self-control

- Weak or no willpower

- An overabundance or lack of self-esteem

- Insecurity

- Fatigue

- Problems with weight control

- Indigestion, gas, or bloating

People who are overly confident often have a midsection that protrudes visibly, making it look like they are strutting their stuff for all to see. But people who have a lack of self-confidence are often seen walking and standing with rolled shoulders, hunched over looking timid or defeated.

Yellow is the color selected for the Solar Plexus Chakra. Yellow as a color is strongly emotional. It gives off a feeling of friendliness and confidence. It brings feelings and thoughts of self-esteem, optimism, and courage. People feel capable, prepared, and stimulated by the color yellow.

The Solar Plexus Chakra rules an individual's sense of self-esteem. This chakra is the chakra of balance and action that focuses on commitment, personal power, and individual willpower. It governs anything to do with the stomach, the digestive system, and the metabolism. A blocked Solar Plexus Chakra will cause a person to suffer from control issues, anger issues, difficulty making decisions, and low self-esteem. This is not limited to just feeling bad about oneself but also might mean a person is easily taken advantage of or often expresses feelings of apathy or indulges in procrastination.

The Fourth Chakra: The Heart Chakra:

The Heart Chakra is said to be the chakra known for expressing caring and love and for nurturing ourselves and other people. It is centrally located in the center of the chest and is balanced by all of the other chakras. The color for the Heart Chakra is green and its element is air. The Heart Chakra corresponds to the circulatory system and to the arms, lungs, and the heart. Its theme is 'to love'. An excessive Heart Chakra or one that is closed or blocked will send out the following symptoms:

- Jealousy

- Grief

- Excessive self-sacrifice

- Loneliness and co-dependency

- A tendency to hold grudges against other people

- Heart disease

- Problems with the circulatory system

- Pain or tightness in the chest

- Problems with the respiratory system

The Heart Chakra is the middle of the seven chakras and in it lays the metaphysical and literal heart of the body. When a person's life is out of harmony, especially when it comes to receiving and giving love, the Heart Chakra can be adversely affected. People will often close their hearts completely when their hearts are hurt by the betrayal of another person, by the love that is not returned, or by crushing grief. While this may seem like a reasonable response it can also cause an interruption in the flow of energy throughout the entire body. Open and unconditional love is what fuels the Heart Chakra.

The color for the Heart Chakra is green, the color of health. Green gives people an overall feeling of good health and well-being. Feelings and thoughts of love, kindness, and compassion follow the color green. Green generally makes people feel empathetic, alert, and healthy.

This chakra is where the spiritual being and the physical being meet inside the body. The Heart Chakra is all about love. It encourages awakening and acceptance of unwavering service, complete forgiveness, and spiritual awareness. When the Heart Chakra is balanced and aligned compassion and love will flow freely in the person's life through receiving love and giving love.

The Fifth Chakra: The Throat Chakra

People honor their own personal truths in the Throat Chakra and express themselves there. It is located in the throat and its balancing lower chakra is the Sacral Chakra. Its color is bright blue and its element is ether. The Throat Chakra corresponds to the thyroid, the jaw, the mouth, the shoulders, the neck, and the throat. Its theme is 'to speak'. If the Throat Chakra is excessive or is closed or blocked it may exhibit the following symptoms:

- Difficulties in communicating with other people

- Pathological lying

- Problems with speaking

- Prolonged periods of silence or excessive talking

- Diseases of the thyroid gland

- Pain in the shoulders

- Discomfort in the throat

- Tightness in the jaw

The Throat Chakra is particularly delicate and excessive comments from others like 'you are wrong' or 'be quiet' can cause damage to this chakra. Having personal expression stifled causes a person to hide deep within oneself or to close off all expression. The Throat Chakra prefers communication that is open and expressed with encouragement and constructively in a safe environment.

The special color for the Throat Chakra is blue which a highly intellectual color is. Blue promotes feelings of trust and intelligence. Feelings and thoughts of duty, communication, and logic go with the color blue. It can easily make a person feel more well-spoken, efficient, and smart.

The Throat Chakra is the first of the chakras that are completely spiritual chakras, as opposed to the lower chakras that are more concerned with the physical aspects of the body. A blocked Throat Chakra will cause a person to have trouble speaking freely. They may also find it difficult to stay focused and to pay attention when others are speaking. It may also cause the person to fear being judged by other people. A closed or blocked Throat Chakra can also cause physical ailments like tension headaches, stiffness in the neck and the shoulders, problems with the thyroid gland, and excessive sore throats.

The Sixth Chakra: The Third Eye

Intuition and deep knowledge lie in the Third Eye Chakra. This chakra can be found in the center of the forehead. Its special color is indigo and its special element is light. Its theme is 'to see' and its corresponding body parts are the pituitary gland, the ears, and the eyes. The Solar Plexus is the balancing chakra. A Third Eye Chakra that acts excessively or is blocked or closed will exhibit the following symptoms:

- Denial of personal intuitive abilities

- Hallucinations or illusions

- Night terrors or nightmares

- Mental confusion

- Headaches

Everyone is naturally born with a type of sixth sense, the ability to use our inner knowledge to scope out different situations and other people. If the Third Eye Chakra gets clouded, then people will fall prey to disillusion or mental confusion. People may also feel as if their feelings are not really their own. A person will need to have an unblocked and fully open Third Eye Chakra in order to be able to embrace their own intuitive abilities that are inherent in everyone.

Indigo, the color of the Third Eye Chakra is a color that is highly spiritual. Indigo gives off feelings of spiritual development and of being wise. It makes people think of feelings and thoughts of peace, self-awareness, and psychic energy. The color indigo makes people feel magical, intuitive, and very wise.

The Third Eye Chakra is also responsible for anything that happens between the outside world and the person. It acts as a bridge between the outside and the person within, allowing people to see the clear picture even though the drama and illusions. If this chakra is blocked the person might have problems with learning new skills, recalling facts that are important, accessing their intuition, or even trusting their own inner voice. Imbalances in the lower chakras will cause the Third Eye Chakra to become imbalanced and will make the person act more introverted, dismissive, and judgmental toward others and their situations. A blocked or closed Third Eye will cause physical issues like dizziness and headaches and mental issues like anxiety and depression.

The Seventh Chakra: The Crown Chakra

The Crown Chakra is the highest in body position of the chakras. It is known to be the source of the divine entity is found and is the person's connection to the spiritual world beyond the self. The chakra is found at the top of the person's head. Its color is white or violet and it has no corresponding element. The Crown Chakra corresponds directly to the pineal gland, which is responsible for regulating all of the hormones in the body, and the cerebral cortex, which is responsible for personality and intelligence, gross and fine motor function, processing language, and the operation of the senses. Its theme is 'to understand' and it is balanced by the Root Chakra. If a Crown Chakra is excessive or closed or blocked it can exhibit the following symptoms:

- Denial of the existence of a God or other Higher Power

- Irrational fear of spirituality, the occult, or mysticism

- Problems with understanding concepts that are spiritual

- An overly opinionated attitude

- Feelings of being disconnected from other people

People become disconnected from the intelligence and the wisdom of their higher selves if the Crown Chakra is blocked or closed. When people are able to accept a connection to an understanding of divine matters then they will be able to enjoy an existence that is more enlightening and fulfilling.

The Crown Chakra has two colors, violet, and white. These are universal colors that promote a feeling of being connected to all people, things, and situations. Violet and white cause people to feel and think of meditation, oneness, and spirituality. People naturally feel more relaxed around violet and white, as well as more spiritually alive and awake, more exalted, and more evolved.

A Crown Chakra that is closed or blocked may give a person great feelings of emotional distress or isolation. They will feel disconnected from the remainder of the world. It is possible to have no ill effects from the Crown Chakra but never be totally able to feel it. Some people feel totally normal but never feel spiritually enlightened or in an exalted state of the connection. This is also quite normal and totally reasonable. The crown chakra is often quite difficult to open and is only fully opened through specific meditative exercises or yoga routines. It may also open only at specific times that it controls by itself and not when the person feels it should be open.

The various chakras are all important to the health of the physical body and the personal psyche at the same time and in the same way. The special function of the chakras in the body is to draw in energy by spinning in order to provide this energy to the physical, emotional, mental, and spiritual health of the body. The system of the chakras is evolving and dramatic, ever-changing while remaining rooted in their position and function.

Chapter 3 Why Chakras are important and what they influence

If you lack the ability to love, which in turn will not enable you to receive it, then how will you survive on this earth, especially if you cannot love yourself? Thriving in this world without friendship or other meaningful relationships that will help and encourage your growth and success in life is impossible, and not just financially speaking. Practicing love is not difficult if you can change a negative mindset into a positive one, starting with taking the time to understand someone else's feelings.

Real love is never fickle. A fickle love is a kind that attaches you to someone or something for so long. Eventually, though, you end up suddenly disliking the object of your love when an associate or friend has an opposing thought about them.

There is a saying that goes "you can't truly love anyone unless you love yourself." While it is good to be charitable and kind to others, you must also take time to repair and take care of yourself. If you have the means to take care of someone else yet leave none for yourself, then you will lose the ability to survive and then become bitter because of it, and that progresses to your love for people turning into the opposite: bitterness and hatred. Those people, in turn, will turn bitter and sometimes hateful towards you in order to defend their well-being and survival.

Another test of genuine love is if and how you will be by that person's side, despite their flaws or the rough patches they experience. For example, if a mother finds out her child has been arrested for a petty crime, such as shoplifting, it is natural for a mother to be very angry with her child, as she did not raise him to steal, but theft is not a reason for her to disown him. She, as the mother, must be able to give guidelines so that he will never shoplift again, and help him down the right path of life to become a successful and worthwhile adult.

Say a close friend or family member becomes ill to the point they must be hospitalized. It's paramount that you have enough free time, and more, to visit them and help them as much as possible until they are nursed back to health enough to return to their normal lives. What's more, you should still keep the bond going, through happy and rough times.

One of the worst things you can do is sever ties with a person if they suddenly become strapped of funds due to a disaster or other crisis. Again, friendships and relationships are not only about happy times and night outs. Severing ties betrays an exploitive spirit, and anyone who uses people for selfish gain automatically loses any and all respect from others.

Another way to show you truly love someone is by forgiving them of their wrongdoings towards you. Forgiveness does take some time, though. However, if this person commits gross wrong, such as murder another loved one or a beloved pet simply out of a fit of rage, then forgiveness can be difficult and near-impossible for you to have. There is always a reasonable balance and medium.

As another saying goes, self-care isn't selfish.

Using Meditation To Help Your Chakras

Meditation works particularly best when done first thing in the morning, in order to have a clear, focused mind for the entire day. In order to have a successful meditation session, though, you need to be in a quiet, private space completely free of distractions and allow yourself to just relax for a few moments. For mediation, you do not have to work on all your chakras at once. In fact, it is best to focus on one that you're struggling with most at that particular moment.

Start by sitting perfectly upright, back straight, sitting Indian style, but be sure you're comfortable. Then close your eyes and focus on the sound and pattern of your breathing. There are specific ways of meditation for each chakra.

For the root chakra, focus your energy on the color red, and think of a red light aura around you. This takes as much time as you personally need.

For the sacral chakra, focus on your inner child and the color orange.

Now, you can move onto the navel chakra and focus on the color yellow and positive ways to deal with criticism from others.

Think of the color green when focusing on the heart chakra and also focus on love, compassion and how you will receive and also transmit those feelings to others in a proper way.

Blue is the color you should have pictured in your mind when your meditation session centers most around the throat chakra. You should also focus on being your own person and how you will use your sense of true self when dealing with the day ahead of you.

Indigo is your spirit color when you move your focus onto the third eye chakra. Your spirit guides here should also be those of wisdom, grip on reality and a positive mindset in order to not only combat whatever obstacle comes your way but to just stay strong in whatever it is you must deal with for the day, both good and bad.

To focus on the crown chakra, focus on your violets as well as a very bright white and focus on living in the present and moving forward and never looking backward.

While it was said earlier that you're not required to work on all the chakras at the same, your meditation session will actually be more beneficial and even more useful if you do work on all of them in one session. However, if you're a novice meditator when it comes to chakras, just work on one or two at a time until you become advanced enough to where you can start working on all of them in one session. Again, also keep in mind that there is no time limit for these kinds of meditation sessions. It is important to take as much time as you know you truly need. Also, remember to never become angry if your meditation doesn't always turn out to be the way you expect it to. Patience must be learned to have a successful and peaceful meditation session.

Yoga is an ancient practice that stems from Eastern cultural and religious practices from thousands of years ago. The history of yoga is heavily wrapped up in the concept of the energy centers, or "nadis" as they are referred to in ancient Sanskrit texts and that as a practicing Yoga involves the concept of working with the whole system, including the chakras.

Western cultures have only known of or explored yoga practices, in the past 50 or so years, and as we embrace these concepts and beliefs systems, we can all begin to appreciate the benefits of this unique and all-encompassing practice.

Yoga is a system and a philosophy that believes in the use of physical postures, breath, diet, and meditation to accomplish the goal of total wholeness, balance, and peace, as well as connection to the divine. It is hard to say exactly when and how it came into being, however, the Vedic texts of the Hindu religions' descriptions of yoga poses, postures, beliefs and concepts were written, and the same knowledge is still widely practiced today all over the world.

There are a number of amazing benefits to practicing yoga and some of them are the following:

- Improves flexibility in the muscles, ligaments, tendons and connective tissues

- Builds and enhances muscle strength when regularly practiced

- Assists in promoting a better posture overall, through the different asanas, or poses that are practiced

- Helps to prevent the breakdown of your cartilage and joint health as you age

- Helps protect the spine by strengthening the body overall, and by creating better flexibility in all areas of the spinal column

- Promotes healthy bones and can help cure or aid osteoporosis, osteoarthritis and other degenerative bone disorders

- Enhances blood flow throughout the whole body, as well as the enrichment of the blood with fresh, oxygenated blood cells because of the breathing exercises involved, allowing for more oxygen to fill your muscles, organs, and joints

- Assists in the pumping of lymph through the lymphatic system, which drains the body of toxins and promotes a healthier immune system

- Promotes a steady and balanced heart rate, whether you are suffering from high or low blood pressure

- Regulates your hormones and gland secretions to allow for a more balanced internal function

- Releases dopamine and serotonin into the brain and bloodstream, creating a higher state of happiness and good feelings

- Helps you consistently engage in a healthier lifestyle because of how it creates a balance and wholeness with all systems of the self

- Will lower your blood sugar when practiced regularly and in accordance with healthier diet and eating habits

- Enhances your ability to stay focused and concentrated

- Improves physical balance

- Relaxes your overall system to help you maintain and healthy functioning nervous system

- Relieves and releases any tension that might be stuck in places around the body, especially when regularly practiced

- Connects you to a deeper, more relaxed sleep state so that you can truly rest and rejuvenate

- Boosts your immune system functions and helps prevent illness

- Opens up your lung capacity, when regularly practiced, to help exercise and stretch the diaphragm, lungs and rib cage

- Can help to prevent digestive system malfunction and disorders, like gastroenteritis and irritable bowel syndrome

- Relieves general pain

That is quite a list of benefits and those are just relating to the physical state of the body. Here are some of the mental and emotional benefits of practicing yoga:

- Helps to promote a sense of calm and peace of mind

- Enhances and develops a sense of self-worth and self-esteem

- Provides a heightened sense of inner strength and willpower

- Can connect you to your intuition, inner guidance, and sometimes spiritual guidance

- Can connect you to a supportive community of like-minded people

- Prevents mental health issues as well as addictions and drug or alcohol abuse

- Helps you to build more personal awareness and provides an opening to personal growth and transformation

- Can have a benefit to your interpersonal relationships, due to the effects of balancing all of the above-mentioned components

- Heals insecurities about the body and mind

- Opens and connects you with your mind's eye, or third eye and intuition

- Promotes compassion, empathy and ability to serve others

- Promotes self-care rituals

As you can see, the benefits of yoga are magnificent, and when you realize that this ancient philosophy was born in the same place as the concept of chakras and how to engage with your whole energetic system, then you might understand why it is so important to understand the usefulness of this practice in healing your chakras.

Whether or not you are already practicing yoga in your daily life, this section of yoga poses is specifically connected to helping you open certain chakras. If you are a beginner with yoga, take it slow and don't worry if it takes time to get the poses right. Listen to your body and work where it feels comfortable. If you are more advanced in yoga, then this will be an overview of which poses you can use to help you heal any blocks.

In general, you don't have to go through these poses in the order they are presented. You may want to work with one pose more closely during a particular chakra healing block with just one or two poses at a time. You can also find videos online of more in-depth Kundalini yoga practices that can help you awaken your whole system through a process or full yoga routine. Feel free to explore the options.

Do what will feel comfortable for your body and feel free to modify any of the seated positions if you feel like you need to sit in a chair or stand. Just listen to your body and your intuition as you work through them. You can use a yoga mat, but it is not required.

The Root Chakra

Crow Pose

1. Take a moment to position your body by standing with your feet about shoulder -width apart, or just slightly wider than that. Imagine that your body is a tree and that roots are growing out of the soles of your feet into the ground while your spine grows taller like a tree trunk reaching up to the sky.

2. Lower your body into a squat that you can sustain, so the back of your thighs will be touching the back of your calves. If you need to maintain balance, you can reach your hands out in front of you while you lower yourself.

3. Pull your arms in so that your elbows are on in the inside of your knees. Hold your hands together, palm to palm, like you are praying. Hold your hands like thin in front of your heart while you work on keeping your spine straight.

4. From this posture, breathe deep, slow breaths into your belly and hold the breath there.

5. Breathe out and totally empty your lungs.

6. Repeat this breathing around 5 times, inhaling and exhaling. If you need to pause and stand up from this position, you can do so, and then try to go back into this

pose a few more times. (it's okay to take breaks until you feel more connected to holding this pose for a longer period of time).

7. After holding this for a bit and repeating the breath cycles, from this squat position, carefully sit your bottom down on the floor and slowly roll back onto your back. Stretch your hips and let your body sink into the floor while you breathe and rest.

8. While you lay on your back, try to let your attention focus on the vibration of your root chakra. How does it feel? Is it more open and awake? Is it vibrating at all?

9. Carefully move into your next pose, or whatever other activities you are planning on doing with your root, or other chakras.

The Sacral Chakra

Bridge Pose

1. Lie down on the floor with your back flat (you can put a pillow under your knees if necessary).

2. Breathe deeply through the nostrils, filling the abdomen first. Exhale as slowly as you can. Repeat this relaxing breath cycle for several rounds to help you relax.

3. When you are ready, gently pull your feet up so that they are flat on the floor and continue drawing them in close to your bottom, but not all the way for your heels to be touching your glutes. Your knees should be pointed toward the sky. You can modify how close you pull your feet in if it is uncomfortable on your knees.

4. Make sure your hands are flat on the floor next to you, arms at your sides. A modification would be to hold onto your ankles if it is possible, or comfortable.

5. Breath in deeply, filling up your abdomen. Bring your hips off the floor and push them up toward the sky. Start with your tailbone and lift one vertebra off the floor at a time. Take it slowly. Try to get to a point where only your shoulders are on the floor, and the soles of your feet and head.

6. Hold this position for a few moments or breaths.

7. When you let the exhale out, lower yourself, one vertebra at a time.

8. Repeat this cycle several times. While you push your hips into the air, imagine your sacral chakra opening wider and flowing more freely. Make sure your breath is what is guiding you up and down. Let all of the blocks

or negative vibrations lift out of you as you lift your hips.

9. Relax down onto the floor and lower your legs. Breathe deeply for several moments before carrying on.

The Solar Plexus

Platform Pose

1. This will be like performing a plank pose, which engages your abdominal and core muscles.

2. Lie down on the floor so that you are belly down. Adjust your palms so that they are aligned with your body next to your pectoral muscles, or shoulders.

3. The tops of your feet should be touching the floor and will remain this way during this pose. For comfort on your foot bones, a yoga mat may be a good choice.

4. Point your toes away from your body and try to keep them in this pose while you work.

5. As you inhale in a long, deep breath, push your body up off of the floor, straightening your arms, like in a Closeout. Keep toes pointed and heels together. You should be in a plank or platform with your body now. (if this is too challenging to start, modify by pushing up from your knees instead of the tops of your feet).

6. Pull your eyes and head down as though you are looking toward your navel.

7. While doing this pose, remember to keep your back, spine, and neck straight.

8. Hold this position and take several deep inhales and exhales. Try to focus on filling your belly all the way before releasing.

9. You can visualize bright, yellow, sunshine light churning in your solar plexus as you hold this pose and breathe.

10. When you are ready, lower yourself, knees first and then push yourself back into a ball. Pull your arms around behind you and place your forehead on, or close to the floor (child's pose). Hold this pose for a while.

11. Repeat steps as many times as you want to.

The Heart Chakra

Camel Pose

1. Kneel down on the floor, but do not sit back on your heels. Keep your thighs and knees in line with your shoulders.

2. Put your hands, palms down, on your low back.

53

3. Take a deep inhale in as you open your chest and push your heart out. Pull your shoulder blades together, as close as they will go, to help you become more open in the front of your chest.

4. Breathe in and out as you hold this pose and try to open wider and wider in your chest. Make sure your breath is filling your abdomen and not going up into your chest.

5. To enhance the openness of your chest, try pushing your hips forward to help your heart point up towards the sky, maintaining support on your low back with your hands.

6. Gently allow your head to tilt back to expose your throat, focusing on keeping your chest and heart open, by pulling your shoulder blades together and opening your front.

7. If it is comfortable to do so, you can drop your hands down behind you to grab your ankles, lowering your head back further. Take it slow and only do what is comfortable.

8. Breathe from here, or the original pose (without holding your ankles) for several cycles of inhaling and exhaling. Let a smile form on your face and bring the heartfelt warmth of your grin to your heart opening pose.

9. At the time you are ready, slowly return your head to its original position and let your body return to an upright pose. Sit back on your heels and place your hands, palms together in front of your heart for a few breath cycles before moving forward with your day.

The Throat Chakra

Cobra Pose

1. Place your body belly down on the floor. Connect your forehead to the ground and make sure that the tops of your feet are also resting on the ground behind you.

2. Align your palms so that they are face down next to your shoulders.

3. Push only your upper body up off of the floor keeping your hips on the ground.

4. Try to keep your shoulders down and neck long as you straighten your arms to push yourself up.

5. If you can, you can try to lift your pelvis off the floor (to keep your back supported), while trying to maintain dropped shoulders and straight arms. You don't want your shoulders up by your ears for this pose.

6. From here, draw in a deep inhale of breath and let your chest puff out a little. While breathing in, tilt your head

back gently to support your neck. This will expose your throat.

7. Keep your arms straightened and try your best not to hyperextend them.

8. You will inhale and exhale from this position for a few cycles.

9. Lower yourself gently to the original position and rest with some inhales and exhales.

10. Repeat steps 1-9 for a few more cycles, or as desired

The Brow Chakra

Pranam Pose

1. You will start by sitting on your heels on the floor, so kneeling back on your heels and feet (you may need to place a pillow under you for comfort if this position is hard for you to relax in for a longer period of time).

2. While you sit in this position, collect yourself and ground your energy through breath. You can use several slow, deep breaths, or you can engage in some alternating nostril breathing.

3. Remember to keep your spine long and straight and as you are breathing in and out, sense your energy rising

56

up through you, all the way from your root, like the Kundalini snake rising up through your chakras.

4. From here, you can spread your knees out a bit so that they are wider in this kneeling position.

5. As you take in a long, deep breath, you will start to lower yourself forward so that you are going toward the floor. Remember to keep your spine straight in this process.

6. Your arms will stretch out in front of you and you will need to try and get your torso as close to the floor as you can without arching your back. This may require widening your knees to open you up for that. Stay loose and relaxed, with an open heart center.

7. Your arms should be stretched ahead of you on the floor, pointing away from your body. Bring your palms together and keep your arms pointed away like this.

8. Allow your body to fully relax into this posture, forehead on the floor, arms stretched out, palms together, torso leaning into the ground. Breath here for as long as you comfortably can (ten minutes is a good measure of time).

9. Imagine your third eye pulsating with indigo light as you breathe in and out several times.

10. Spend time here listening to your inner mind and intuition. Allow any visions to come forth and practice "going within".

11. As you feel ready to move forward, you can pull your hands closer to your body and push yourself slowly up off of the floor to come back to a kneeling position.

12. Spend time assimilating to your upright posture with breath and meditation.

13. Repeat this pose if you need to, or move forward with your next activity.

The Crown Chakra

Prasad Pose

1. You can start this pose exactly as you did with the previous pose (Pranam Pose).

2. Take time to center yourself with your breath. Spend as long as you need to just sit on your heels with your breath to connect to yourself and your energy.

3. As if you are scooping water out of a pool, bring your hands toward you and make a bowl shape. Keep your hands cupped like this, together and touching, held in front of your heart center.

4. Consider this hand placement like a living-bowl of sacred energetic reception. How you hold your hands is

how you are ready to receive. This is where you can pull the light of the divine into your heart.

5. Try to keep your body soft and relaxed while you are holding your hands in this way. Relax the tension in your arms, neck, shoulders, and back.

6. Breathe deeply and slowly and smile.

7. See a beam of light pouring into your living-bowl. You can visualize this with your open third eye. This is the energy of Universal love pouring into your cup. Allow yourself to reflect on the energy of "all-ness" and feeling enlightened, or full of this light energy.

8. Practice this state of mind for several minutes while you breathe and visualize.

9. Keep your eyelids soft and gently open. Focus your eyes toward the tip of your nose. This action will bring you closer to your third eye will you place yourself in an opening with the divine of your crown energy. This can feel awkward if you are not used to it, so practice going back and forth with your "nose gazing."

10. Breath only through the nose, both inhales and exhales, for a while.

11. When you are ready to change poses or positions, bring your hands down to your lap and hold them palms up to continue receiving as you focus on returning to the present moment and moving forward in the day.

All of these poses are presented in a way to make it easy and fun for you to start engaging in the physicality of connecting with your chakras and opening them up to the healing process. The more often you do these poses, the more you will feel the shifts and transformations in your energy. Doing each of them only once will not have a lasting or long-term impact on your healing journey. In order to allow for true healing, it is best to develop a regular routine to help you engage with the power of opening your chakras and preventing yourself from falling back into old energetic cycles.

The best way to use them is through your own intuitive process, however, when you are just getting started, you can begin with these yoga poses by stringing them together into one, fluid routine, starting at the root and then going all the way up to the crown. You can even take it back down to the root again, and end with a final Prasad pose. This activity will engage your whole chakra system and help you maintain a focus on the whole body, mind, and spirit as you work on healing your chakras from bottom to top and back down again.

The energy that you put into yoga and the healing energy of these poses is the energy you will get back. It has been proven that yoga shifts and transforms your whole being into a state of calm, relaxation, whole health, and presence of mind. Bringing these yoga poses in your every day or weekly rituals for healing your energy are sure to bring you closer to your energy faster.

Earth Star Chakra (Vasundhara) And Soul Star Chakra (Sutara)

Apart from a physical body, we also have an etheric body. This is the energy field around us. It is a well-known fact that we all have an energy body all around us. This energy field is very important when we are trying to balance and empower the energy chakras inside our body. When we go into a meditative state, our energy field becomes weak and volatile as we are trying to balance the flow of energy. This can give the energies outside our body a chance to penetrate. This can get dangerous as we can't have control over the kind of energies present around us. To ensure that you remain safe and able to reach the meditative state easily, it is important that you work toward strengthening the Earth Star Chakra (Vasundhara) and the Soul Star Chakra (Sutara).

Earth Star Chakra (Vasundhara)

The literal meaning of Vasundhara in Sanskrit is earth or the world. This chakra is not present inside the body but around 12-18 inches under your feet. Strengthening this chakra is important for grounding yourself properly and ensuring that negative energies around you don't penetrate your energy field.

The earth star chakra is directly connected to the root chakra or Muladhara. It is the keeper of the karmic cycles. The earth is the witness to everything done by us in this life, as well as the past lives. Therefore, our Karma is always there. It can have a deeper impact on our lives, for which we may not be prepared. Strengthening the earth star chakra helps in preventing the harm from negative energies arising even from our past actions.

A strong earth star chakra helps in natural healing. It also transmutes negative energies around us. If your earth star chakra is strong, you will feel grounded and will be able to focus better on meditation and balancing of other chakras.

The best way to strengthen the earth star chakra is to do tree meditation. It helps you in getting connected to your roots. The color of this chakra is brown and black. Jet, onyx, and black tourmaline are the gems that can help in strengthening your earth star chakra. You can also use essential oils like black peppercorn, white ceremonial sage, and myrrh for healing your earth star chakra.

Soul Star Chakra (Sutara)

The literal meaning of Sutara in Sanskrit is 'very bright.' This chakra is located 6-12 inches above your head. It is just above the crown chakra but outside your body. This chakra is very important as it helps you in establishing a deep connection with higher energies.

The soul star chakra is also called the seat of the soul. Scriptures state that this chakra opens the portal to higher realms. It is also the gateway through which the soul enters your body at the time of birth and leaves the body at the time of death to get mixed with the eternal energy.

Strengthening the soul star chakra can help you in establishing a connection with enlightened beings. You will be able to interact with positive energy forms that are beyond our realm. This chakra is a point of deep relaxation and comfort. By strengthening this chakra, you can ensure peace and tranquility in your life. You will feel more alive and blissful.

The color of this chakra is mauve. The best way to strengthen this chakra is to meditate. You can also wear gems like optical calcite, rainbow moonstone, and scolecite. Essential oils like the white lotus, gardenia, and elemi are also helpful in balancing this chakra.

The Influence Of Chakras On Our Physical Health

We know that chakras are not present inside our body physically.

They are centers where the energy is present in concentrated form. These centers channelize the energy to various other parts of the body. A chakra is a vortex of energy. It is constantly in motion and runs on a very delicate balance. However, In spite of chakras not being physically present in the body, they have a deep impact on our mental, emotional, spiritual, as well as physical health. This mystery has kept the scientists baffled.

However, now it is a known fact that chakras have a deep impact on our endocrine system. The seven chakras influence the seven endocrine glands present along our spinal cord. The endocrine glands are ductless glands that act as the main control mechanism of our body. They produce hormones that can affect our functioning and health to a great extent.

The chakras directly influence the glands that are responsible for producing hormones. An imbalance in the chakras also affects our glands and their functioning.

If there is an imbalance in our chakras, it can have serious health implications as it would affect the subsequent gland under its sphere of influence. Our immune system is also a part of it; hence, imbalance in the chakras also affects your immunity.

Chakras And Nadis

Vedas says that there are 72000 main 'Nadis' or nerves in our body that are connected with millions of other nadis. On this Nadi system, there are 144 important junction points, and these junction points, as you have probably guessed, are known as chakras. So, there are 144 chakras in our body located at various crucial junction points in our body. They control the functioning and energy transfer in the body.

It is important to remember that nerves are only transferring information in the form of energy. The chakras regulate this energy transfer to a great degree. It is mentioned in the Vedas that out of these 144 nadis 142 have a physical presence, whereas the two chakras don't have a physical presence. You don't need to do anything in order to balance these two chakras. If all the other chakras are functioning smoothly, these two chakras will function well on their own.

We further divide the remaining 142 chakras into seven major energy groups. These are called the seven major chakras. These seven chakras then govern our physical, mental, emotional, and spiritual growth through the intricate endocrine system and nervous system or the system of nadis.

The chakras may look like a mythical concept, but they physically manifest themselves as energy centers that can affect our overall functioning to a great degree.

Space, or rather the entire Universe, is composed of energy. Science explains time and time again that energy is what makes up all living and non-living things. Essentially, energy is a reality. This includes your body. There is a host of electrical and energetic impulses coursing through your body all the time. It is this energy that reacts to the energy around you, as well as reacting to the Universal energy. The chakras are conduits for being able to align well with the Universe and the world around you.

Those that have reached Samadhi, or the highest level of enlightenment, are the few that have found the balanced joy of having completely balanced chakras at all times. Most people will not know this feeling. Instead, you will struggle like the rest of us, finding ease in some situations when the chakras are clearer, while other times, those same situations seem like a chore. The good news is that when you notice a chakra or two is imbalanced or not aligned, you can do some things about it. The hard thing is that your misaligned chakras will not be jumping for joy as you work to find balance. Healing yourself and fixing your chakras can be a mental challenge, if not physically challenging as well. Listed below are some of the great benefits of having aligned chakras, and more reasons why you should look to heal and balance your energy centers.

1. Your physical health and well-being

Your life force, or prana, or energy, is moved through your body through the nadis. This energy courses through your body, passing through certain centers or "stations," known as your chakras. Similar to how you want to exercise and eat a good diet to help keep your arteries clear for proper blood flow, you want to do certain things to keep your chakra centers clear for proper energy flow. Imbalances or blockages occur during your normal, everyday life. For example, when you experience fear or negative emotions, you block energy flow. Also, if you have unhealthy lifestyle habits, you block your life force. Finding a balance in your chakras means you are able to better balance your spiritual, emotional, mental, and physical health.

2. Your spiritual well-being

Just like your physical health, your spiritual well-being is important for ideal functioning in the world today. Being connected spiritually helps ensure you are calm and stable in your thoughts and actions. You receive energy from the spiritual realm first. It travels down into your body resulting in your mental and emotional experiences and, finally, your physical experience. This is why it is so important to address your spiritual health by balancing your chakras. This connection impacts all areas of your life. Your physical body and the spiritual realm are connected through your chakras. Making sure this relationship is balanced ensures your body is balanced. Typically, while balancing your chakras, you begin at the bottom and move to the top. This is like walking up a ladder from the bottom to the top, instead of trying to jump to the top of the ladder and ignore all the missing steps below. When you are successful at unblocking your chakras, your energy can flow freely in from the spiritual realm, balancing all aspects of your life. Only those that master their crown chakra can attain enlightenment or Samadhi. This is according to the Ashtanga yoga philosophy, as outlined by Maharishi Patanjali, a well-known Indian sage.

3. Throwing out bad energy stored up in your body

Finding balance in your chakras means also finding balance in your mind and heart, as well. You live a healthier life, not because you are physically fit, but because you support your emotional and mental well-being. Clearing out negative energy blocked in these energy centers allows you to open up to healthier relationships, handle financial matters more effectively, and more. The waste that needs to be "recycled" from your everyday life needs to be removed. The more often you clear out this "bad" energy from your body, the clearer and more relaxed you will feel.

4. Bring in more joy and love into your life

It may sound obvious that the Heart chakra is related to your ability to receive and give love; however, in order for you to feel joy and deep acceptance of yourself, you also need a clear second chakra or the sacral chakra. This is the place of true purpose and identity. Your heart is necessary for love, but your sacral chakra is necessary for fulfillment and vitality in your life. Sometimes, when this second chakra is blocked, you feel disconnected from your purpose, unsure about what you should do, lack creativity, and get overwhelmed emotionally. Those with a balance in this area often appreciate beauty and art and are typically more spontaneous. When you are searching for your purpose and happiness in life, it is wise to focus on clearing this center.

5. Connecting to your inner self

Like mentioned in the last concept, you need to clear your second chakra to accept who you are and become clear on your purpose in this life. This acceptance and clarity bring about joy and love. But you also need to heal and clear your first chakra to get a full appreciation of your true self. Your human body, or "mortal coil," is a tool for your soul's experience. The more you are connected to your inner self, or your soul, the better you understand this existence. This human body you reside in is a small piece of the Divine. Your aim in this world is to connect with the divine consciousness. When you understand this, you are able to detach from material objects and remove negative feelings like jealousy, greed, and anger. All of those negative attributes depress who you really are. Clearing them out of the way, freeing up your first and second chakra to disseminate energy properly, allows you to know your potential and tap into the consciousness of the Universe to live your destined life.

6. Turn the weakness into strength

A chakra shuts down or blocks out negative experiences and feelings. Depending on the situation, it may shut down completely and need a "jumpstart." Sometimes, when you get stuck in a negative pattern, you keep this chakra closed off, not allowing you to grow and develop. Instead, when you unblock those affected chakras, you encourage the energy to flow in and out once more. When your system works properly, you have the ability to turn your negative experiences into positive ones, learn from situations and turn bad habits or patterns into positive results. This is true and sustainable growth, but is only achievable when you are open, clear, and flowing.

7. Improve your finances

One of the amazing benefits of clearing and balancing your chakras is your ability to manifest good things into your life. It is changing the negative and pessimistic views and comments into positive affirmations and requests. When you shift your focus on bringing to you what you need and releasing the things that no longer serve you, you are able to increase your access to the Universal intelligence and bring things to you that you need. This can be in the form of financial assistance. For example, repeating a daily, positive affirmation calling for money to manifest in your life through different revenue streams, you will see it come to fruition when you need it. Money is a common block for your chakras. It is a stress and a negative influence. Your financial matters sit in your first and second chakras, so clearing this block from there is necessary to a properly balanced system. To help you manifest positive financial matters into your life, make sure your first and second chakras are clear and choose a daily affirmation to call forward your financial needs.

8. Turn your desires and wishes into your reality

When you are balanced and healed, you have access to your true purpose and potential. It is only then that you are able to bring your physical body in line with your mental body. This alignment creates a pathway for you to transform your life. It is this connection that allows you to accomplish your goals in life. You change your weaknesses or challenges into strengths and opportunities. You can bring to life all that you desire because it is what you are supposed to do.

9. Improves your intuition

You have a little voice inside of you guiding you along this journey. This voice is your intuition and knows what your purpose is and what you need to do. The problem is that many people learn over time to ignore or suppress this voice. As you tap into understanding your true self, you give space for this voice to be heard. And the more you clear and connect with your Crown and Heart chakra, the better you are at calling forth this intuition when you need it. This is different than waiting for the voice to speak, but rather encouraging the voice to start sharing. To help you tap into this intuition or internal guidance system, make sure you have your body and mind connected. Allow yourself to calm down and be still. Turn your thoughts to positive affirmations and intentions. Give yourself permission to release from your body and soul anything that no longer serves you. Anything that ruins your peace and suppresses your true self is not useful now and should be let go. When you are in this place, allow the positive energy to enter and circulate through your body and all the negative blocks leave your body.

10. Learn how to express your emotions in a good way

Some people are great at revealing how they are feeling, but do so in a way that is overwhelming, or others struggle with showing their emotions and end up with either intense outbursts or complete shutdown. Sharing emotions is good and necessary, but it needs to be done in a calm and balanced manner. As you balance your chakras, you encourage positive energy to enter your body and negative energy to leave. As you do this, you allow negative emotions to be released. This helps remove the blocks in your energy centers. Sometimes, these emotions that you release are hard to express, but when you can release them, you can find a sense of completeness emotionally and physically. Once you let these emotions go, and feel through them, you are able to have a more balanced emotional state. You are more easily able to let go of anxiety, worry, sadness, anger, etc. Even stress is easier managed when your body is balanced mentally and physically. Stress is one of the leading causes of disease, so learning how to let this go is also vital to your physical health.

The Seven Major Chakras and Their Benefits

When one or more is blocked, you will receive messages from your body about it. If you are aware of these messages, you can act quickly on it to bring your body back into balance. Below is a breakdown of some of the benefits of the individual chakras on the body. More details for each chakra and finding balance will be shared later in this book as well. Keep in mind that some of the imbalances are either caused by an underactive or overactive chakra. This is why you will see something like not emotional and overly emotional on the list for what you would feel for an unbalanced chakra.

Your Root Chakra

If you are unbalanced, you feel:

- Insecure
- Unstable
- Insensible
- Unbalanced
- Afraid
- Nervous
- Attached to material items
- greedy

If you are balanced, you feel:

- Trusting
- Connected to community
- Connected to the physical body
- Secure

- Provided for

Your Sacral Chakra

If you are unbalanced, you feel:

- Insensitive
- Unemotional
- Not able to open up to others
- Overly emotional
- Promiscuous

If you are balanced, you feel:

- Sexual
- Accepted
- Confident
- Joyful
- Able to express emotions in a healthy and proper manner

Your Solar Plexus Chakra

If you are unbalanced, you feel:

- Indecisive
- Passive
- Aggressive
- Embarrassed about yourself

If you are balanced, you feel:

- Confident about yourself
- Certain in your thoughts and actions

Your Heart Chakra

If you are unbalanced, you feel:

- Cold
- Not kind or friendly towards others
- Heart palpitations or heart attack
- Jealousy
- Hatred
- Anger
- Grief and excessive sadness
- Fear

If you are balanced, you feel:

- A healthy state of appropriate sadness
- Forgiveness
- Awareness
- Caring
- Empathy
- Compassion
- Healthy relationships
- Peace
- Love for others and for yourself

Your Throat Chakra

If you are unbalanced, you feel:

- Lying
- Unable to talk or clearly communicate
- Shy
- Low self-esteem or self-confidence
- Bad listener
- Talks to much

If you are balanced, you feel:

- Confident in your self
- Able to share your thoughts and feelings clearly
- Creative
- Communicative
- Good at listening
- Honest to others and to their self

Your Third Eye Chakra

If you are unbalanced, you feel:

- Confused
- No imagination
- Overactive imagination
- Living in a fantasy world all the time
- Unaware of others emotions and mental states
- Not smart or intellectual

If you are balanced you feel:

- Intuitive
- Clear-headed
- Intellectual
- Wise
- Spiritual

Your Crown Chakra

If you are unbalanced, you feel:

- Rigid
- Thoughts are inflexible
- Depressed
- Bored
- Greedy
- Frustrated

If you are balanced, you feel:

- Connected to something larger than your self
- Engaged
- Content
- Awake
- Energetic
- Wise
- Satisfied

Chapter 4 Chakras And Auras

Auras are bio-magnetic fields of energies that surround us and are our energy blueprint. It can extend from several feet to a few inches.

Auras just like chakras can also be seen during meditations, with the inner eye, with psychic perception or healing sessions. Both aura and chakra can also be seen with the naked eye after more focus, training, meditation, and learning the knowledge of the human energy field. There are also those people who can see chakra or aura without training. There are also those who take time before been able to get spiritual power to view aura even after years of training.

Auras, just like chakras, can be separated into several other elements. It is easy to know the moods of certain people if you have an idea of what color to relate to their moods without even reading or examining their minds.

Auras enable you to observe the energy of love merging between two couples in love. Two arguing friends will have their energy focused on energy and their auras get thinner. There are several auric or energy fields which make up the auras which include:

Physical Field – Human beings can observe without training and changes based on your health and well-being.

Etheric Field – Changes based on the flow of energy and handles the exchange of energy between the physical body and universal energy.

Emotional Field – Affected by tension and stress

Mental Field – Changes depending on your focus or confusion. it is around your crown head.

The Astral Field – Is the energy field is existing on its own plane free from confines of space and time. The work is done on all chakras to heal and perform their functions appropriately benefit the astral field.

The Etheric Template Field – It is responsible for representing our physical being in the spirit plane.

The Celestial Field – Represents the etheric field as a template in the physical plane. It's super energetic and has access to all the energies offered by the universe.

Casual Field – Has everything to do with the outcome of your life's direction. It is similar to the mental field, but it works on a spiritual plane. It directs our existence in the lower levels based on the universe with no confines of time and space.

There is also a belief that young children have extra-sensory perceptions which enable them to see auric layers and chakras. However, they later shut down these unique powers after adults tell them they see something that does not exist. The children experience these powerful techniques because of the need to connect more with the environment they perceive does not support their involvement or with their physical existence.

Chakra and aura are connected very deeply since the aura produces out the information into the world where your chakras. Your root chakra makes you feel safe and grounded, and this will be projected out in the aura. On the other hand, if your solar plexus feel insecure and weak, you will project this feeling to the world. The aura is a blend of all the information your chakras send out and when your spiritual connection, emotional health and mood change, your colors change as well. However, for chakra's color, they remain constant and are deeply anchored. The color of the chakra can only change if a major event occurs.

Both chakras and auras constitute the individual's spiritual colors. They are also important to the health of a human being. The two channels of energy can also get blocked when the individual is suffering from illness or stress and affect the general health of a person. Specific forms of yoga, meditations, Reiki, and other scientific methods are practiced to purify auras and open blocked chakras to restore good health and the general well-being. The thickness, size, and shape of the chakras and auras describe many things about an individual. The more powerful and strong the aura is, the more fascinating the person, the clear (spacious-thickness-openness) your chakra, the healthier and stronger the person.

Both auras and chakras are capable of revealing a particular disease affecting an individual. When both chakras and auras are weak, it becomes hard to deal with present life situations unless the energies are treated.

Becoming One With Everything Through The Crown Chakra

The third eye chakra may be the most well-known chakra point on the body, but it is not the last chakra point that there is. The seventh and final chakra point on the body is known as the crown chakra. Similar to the throat and third eye chakras in the sense that it seeks enlightenment from a higher power, the crown chakra provides the soul with complete access to any and all realms of existence that are beyond this one. While the throat and third eye chakras can provide the soul with glimpses into the unknown, the crown chakra completely unifies our souls with everything. Think about that for a moment. Everything. Total integration with the universe has also been described as a state of eternal blissfulness or Nirvana.

Basic Information Regarding the Crown Chakra

In Sanskrit, the crown chakra best translates to the word "Sahasrara." Taken literally, Sahasrara means a thousand petals. The symbol for the crown chakra demonstrates this meaning. It is located at the crown of the head, slightly above the end of the forehead. This chakra allows the soul to identify all that is sacred in the world, and become one with it. It can provide the soul with ecstasy, bliss, and freedom from any and all patterns that exist in the world. For example, in some schools of religion, it's thought that our souls are reincarnated from one life into another after the physical body dies. From this school of thought, it's understood that when the crown chakra opens, the soul is no longer to go through the process of reincarnation. Instead, it will transcend all physical forms of consciousness, and become One with the universe.

Purple, the Sahasrara Chakra's Color

While purple is formally the color that is associated with the Sahasrara chakra, white is sometimes interchangeably used to describe this seventh chakra point. Purple is meant to signify connectedness, birth, and rejuvenation. Purple is also meant to signify a reconciling of all feelings of separateness within yourself and with others. In modern and ancient culture, purple is also often associated with distinction, wisdom, or royalty. A healthy crown chakra allows the mind to think deeply, curiously, and without limit. This is what the color purple represents, and why it is associated with the crown chakra. It's also interesting to note that all of the chakras that are found in the head are linked to similar color patterns.

The Pituitary Gland and the Crown Chakra

If you remember, the pituitary gland is responsible for controlling and maintaining the other glands that make up the endocrine system. It's located towards the base of the brain. Unlike the pineal gland which is located closer to the front and center of the brain, the pituitary gland is further from the mind's eye. This suggests that the crown chakra, while similar to the third eye chakra in a few ways, is far more interested in aligning its energy with the unimaginable and mystical than the third eye is.

Your Emotions and the Crown Chakra

One of the reasons why the crown chakra is considered to be the last primary chakra point on the body is because all other chakras must be in balance before this one can even think about opening. Now that you've learned about what it takes to balance all of the six other chakra points on the body, you can probably imagine that this is not an easy task to take on. When the crown chakra is open and flowing, it means that this energy is moving through all of the chakra points throughout the body. Prana is flowing freely, and this allows the body to remain in a state that is constantly rooted in the present moment. When your mind isn't busy thinking about the past and how it's influencing the present and the future, you're able to truly find a greater sense of freedom. Specifically, opening all of the chakras and finally opening the crown chakra will provide you with freedom from attachment, time, and ultimately the limiting aspects of your human form.

Symptoms of an Unbalanced Crown Chakra

An overactive crown chakra will likely exhibit this overzealousness in some of the following ways:

Feeling completely disconnected from the body. You can't seem
- to relate to the physical body that you're in, and this leads to never
being able to feel grounded in your own skin

- Keeping all of your thoughts in your head, rather than expressing
them to other people

- Forgetting to take responsibility for things that are still important
to your earthly existence, such as car payments or keeping
appointments

On the other hand, an underactive crown chakra might manifest
itself in the following ways:

- Having little or no direction in life

- Sensing an inability to set goals for yourself and see them through

- Developing nerve pain or neurological disorders of one kind or
another

- Developing depression, schizophrenia or Alzheimer's disease

- Frequently experiencing headaches

How to Unclog the Crown Chakra

While unpacking the crown chakra to allow for a greater flow of energy is not necessarily easy, there are still plenty of habits that you can cultivate and practice in your daily life if you'd like to work towards that end. Firstly, chanting OM is a great way to stimulate the energy that is found in the crown chakra. You can either chant OM once, or you can also choose to chant it three times in a row. OM is a word that represents universal peace, and universal energy. It also represents a small piece of matter that exists within every energetic being and connects one of us to all of us. Chanting OM reminds us that our enemies and our friends alike all possess at least one piece of humanity that is exactly the same as ours. More importantly, chanting OM reminds us that there is a higher power, regardless of the exact form that it takes.

Chapter 5 Chakras, vortices of energy and light

Now, it's time to start awakening your chakras.

It is important that you awaken your chakras before you use them for your own healing. All people have chakras in their body; these points aren't just active. A re-birthing session must take place first before you awaken your chakras. During the re-birthing stage, you have to exhale in a relaxed way. Visualize that the air you breathe is passing through your chakra points.

1. Root Chakra:

To awaken your root chakra, first, stand with your feet wide apart. Make sure that you are comfortable. Next, rotate your hips from right to left. Do this about 48 to 50 times. Breathe deeply as you rotate your hips, and take three directed breaths when you're done. Repeat the same procedure (hip rotation) from left to right. Follow this with three directed breaths.

2 & 3. Navel Center Chakra:

Just like in the root chakra, take 49 to 50 re-birthing breaths and then tuck your stomach in sharply. You don't want to harm yourself when you get started with this one, but do draw your stomach back a little bit to help you to work on the navel center chakra. This will make a big difference in how much you will be able to feel this particular chakra.

4. Heart Chakra:

Awaken your heart chakra by stretching your arms sideways. Take 49 re-breathing breaths whole moving your arms in a circular manner. Move your arms up and down, and then take three directed breaths. Repeat the process.

5. Throat Chakra:

Drop your head forward and then do a head roll, first to the left, then to the back, and then forward. As you move your head, breathe deeply. You must be able to have 7 re-birthing breaths after each head roll.

6. Third Eye:

Empower your third eye by taking 49 re-birthing breaths and raising your eyebrows quickly as you open your eyes. After that, close your eyes and concentrate on your breathing.

7. Crown Chakra:

Raise your arms as you take seven directed breaths. Feel the energy and imagine it encircling you from head to foot.

Balancing Your Chakras

Balancing your seven chakras is important because when one of your chakras is not balanced, your emotions and your body might be affected. When you are with someone who is sad or happy, it is highly possible for you to channel these emotions. You become a magnet of energy! However, too much bad energy could weaken your state, and you could feel ill. Be responsible for your own emotions. The information below will guide you as to what happens when there is an imbalance in your emotions:

Anger gives you flashes of red. This is such a strong energy that emanates from a person – too much of it is bad for your body as it absorbs other negative elements. When you are angry, know that there is a chakra imbalance in the solar plexus. You also see flashes of red; perhaps this is where the expression "seeing red" came from.

On the other hand, being defensive puts armors or cords around you. Defensiveness signals an imbalance in your brow and solar plexus chakras. Whenever this happens, you feel that you want to alienate yourself from other people. You dislike relationships and reject pieces of advice and help from friends and relatives.

Resentment clouds your vision. Almost similar to anger, resentment makes you unable to think clearly. Making decisions is also difficult for you. There is definitely an imbalance in the heart and solar plexus. The same thing happens when you are really sad. It's like there is a cloud before your eyes. This means there is an imbalance in your heart and crown chakras. Address this quickly. Otherwise, you could feel depressed and anxious.

Jealousy, in contrast, enables hooks of energy to trap you. You feel angry and resentful at the same time. You want to pour your energy into things that aren't worth your time – being jealous. You also become possessive of people. Remember that there is an imbalance of the heart, solar plexus and brow plexus. Lastly, hysteria results in fragmentation. You feel disconnected. There will be times when you can't explain and express what you feel. Communication is difficult. Hysteria is the worst form of emotional and auric disturbance; hence, all the chakras are affected.

Bringing Back the Balance to Your Chakras

To rebalance your chakras, first, you have to create a sacred space for yourself. You could use natural elements here; either surround yourself with the elements that represent fire, water, wind, and earth; or you use your crystals and gemstones to create a sacred circle. Sprinkle salt around the sacred circle to purify it. Next, ground yourself and connect with the energy of the earth. A simple way to do this is to lie on the floor.

Connect with the cosmic energy as well. Imagine that there is a golden energy or a yellow light surrounding you. This light comes from your crown chakra, passes to your heart chakra region, then to your hands. Imagine this light going down to your toes.

Say an affirmation or a prayer to invite your spirit guide, or to at least welcome the cosmic energy. You could start with the "I Have the Right" affirmation. Since the chakras are connected to your body and your emotions, you can say this prayer and mantra. Breathe deeply and concentrate as you say these statements:

I have the right to basic needs.

I feel that my basic needs will be fulfilled soon.

I have the right to feel safe and valued.

I have the right to feel nurtured.

I have the right to address my desires.

I have the right to make decisions for myself.

I have the right to say no to things I don't want to do.

I have the right to love freely.

I have the right to be loved.

I have the right to feel that I am loved.

I have the right to communicate the truth.

I have the right to enjoy the world.

I have the right to fulfill my dreams.

I have the right to learn what the Higher Being teaches.

The next step is to scan the aura thrice. Do this with your dominant hand, as you lie on your back. Start at the top of the head, then use your hand to go over your body down to your feet. Be sensitive to where your chakras are blocked. If you feel any difficulty, use your pendulum to do that for you.

Note on pendulums: Any necklace will do, actually, but it is best to use a crystal dangling from a necklace. Use your intuition when choosing a pendulum.

Open your chakras using your dominant hand. Imagine a golden light coming from your hand and use it to go over your body. Spin your dominant hand 3 times to scan your aura. This will get rid of your blockages. Lastly, the pendulum will guide you to where your energies are blocked. As you hold the pendulum upright, say "I am now testing the ___ chakra. Is this blocked?" Make sure that you have assigned certain movements as responses (i.e. swinging back and forth as "yes" and rotating counterclockwise as "no".

When the pendulum says that, there are areas that are blocked, use your hand to balance the chakra point. Move your hand on top of the blocked region and imagine the golden light from your hands cleansing the area blockage. After moving your hand across the blocked chakra point, refer to your pendulum to check if the blockage has been removed.

If the chakra point has been opened, seal the positive energy by spinning the golden light from your hands on that chakra point three times, counterclockwise. Sweep your hand from the top of your head down to your feet to seal the auras. When you are done, cross your arms over your chest and thank your spirit guides.

Chakras, Endocrine System And The Immune System

In addition to the benefits mentioned earlier, there are many things that chakras control including the efficient functioning of our endocrine system and our emotions. Let us look at each in a bit of detail:

Let us start by recalling the 7 primary chakras and their locations:

1. Root Chakra – situated at the base of the spine

2. Sacral Chakra – situated below the navel

3. Solar Plexus Chakra – situated above the navel

4. Heart Chakra – situated in the middle of the chest

5. Throat Chakra – situated in the throat

6. Third Eye Chakra – situated at the center of the forehead

7. Crown Chakra – situated at the top of the head

The Endocrine System

Next, let us look at the Endocrine System in our body. The Endocrine System is our body's central mechanism of control. It consists of many ductless glands that are responsible for secreting, producing, and distributing different kinds of hormones required for various physiological functions of our body.

These hormones are directly sent through the bloodstream to the places that need them. Effective functioning of the Endocrine System is essential for overall good physical and mental health. The Endocrine System consists of the following elements:

The Pineal Gland – The most important hormone secreted by this gland is melatonin that is responsible for maintaining and regulating your body's circadian rhythm or the internal biological clock. This cone-shaped gland along with the pituitary gland regulates and balances the entire biological and glandular functioning in our body. The third eye chakra can be activated optimally when the pineal and the pituitary glands work perfectly in tandem.

The Pituitary Gland – Also referred to as the 'master gland,' the pituitary gland controls the activities and functioning of most other glands. Attached to the hypothalamus (between the eyes), the pituitary gland regulates the functioning of other organs and other glands. It communicates via signals in different forms.

This pea-shaped gland works in tandem with the pineal gland controls and balances the overall smooth functioning of our body's physiological and biological activities. The energy of the third eye chakra can be released when these two glands are well synchronized with each other.

Pancreas – The two kinds of hormones produced by the pancreas are needed for two basic functions; one to aid in digestion and the other to control energy levels in our body.

Ovaries – These glands produce the female hormones namely progesterone and estrogen and also produce and release eggs for reproduction.

Testes – These glands come in pairs and are responsible for the production and release of the male hormone, testosterone. They also produce and release sperms.

Thyroid – A very important gland, the thyroid is responsible for regulating the heart rate, the metabolic rate and also controls a few digestive functions along with bone maintenance, muscle control, and brain development. The thyroxin produced by the thyroid controls the rate at which our body converts stored food into energy for use. A malfunctioning thyroid can be quite a debilitating factor that comes in the way of a leading a happy life for anyone.

Parathyroid – This gland controls calcium levels in the bloodstream so that the muscles and the nerves function smoothly. The parathyroid also helps in keeping bones healthy and strong.

Hypothalamus – This gland responds to multiple external and internal factors and triggers various reactions to enable stability and a consistent state in our body. The hypothalamus triggers various physiological reactions in response to feelings of hunger, the temperature of your body, feelings of excessive eating, blood pressure, and others. Based on these conditions, it sends signals to other glands and organs to respond appropriately to these triggers to enable a stable and consistent condition of your body.

Adrenal Glands – These glands secrete different kinds of hormones referred to as 'chemical messengers' which travel through the bloodstream to triggers physiological and chemical reactions in various organs.

The Immune System

Millions and millions of cells come together and waltz together in perfect harmony exchanging critical information thereby triggering appropriate and important physiological, biological, and chemical reactions in our body. The cells of the immune system help organs and organ systems in our body to function smoothly helping us live a happy and peaceful life.

Moreover, those cells that are not performing optimally are retired and new ones are automatically generated to take their place thereby enhancing our health and our longevity. If these weak cells are not correctly replaced in the immune system, they end up sending erroneous signals to all parts of the body resulting in disorders and discomforts such as weak digestion, general body weakness and delayed recovery from even simple illnesses.

The way modern medicines work to set this right is by suppressing the action of the well-functioning cells too until such time all the cells do not achieve the same level of functioning. The medication is continued until all the cells in the immune system get back into the synchronized dancing pattern. This is where chakra healing can help in getting our immune system in order.

The Thymus Gland – It is an important gland to be included in this chapter because of it is very closely related to the immune system. It plays an important role in the production of T-cells which form an essential part of the white blood cells that form the core of our immune system. In fact, if you speak to any chakra healer, he or she will tell you the dance of the immune system is the most beautiful and well-coordinated dance in our body.

Chakras and Glands

If you notice the locations of the glands, you will see that they are more or less placed close to different chakras. Although the traditional systems do not speak about the connection between chakras and glands, the modern followers and experts started outlining clear connections between the various chakras, glands, organs and the immune system of the body.

Each chakra is connected to different glands of the endocrine system and facilitates the smooth functioning of that particular gland. Here is a list of the various chakras, the glands they regulate, their functions and the signs of warnings associated with an inefficiently functioning gland/chakra.

Root Chakra – This is connected to the adrenal glands and stands for self-preservation and physical energy. The issues that the root chakra and the adrenal glands handle are associated with survival and security. In the males, the sacral chakra is closely linked to the gonads. The fight/flight response of the adrenal glands located at the top of the kidneys is directly connected to the survival drive of the root chakra.

A weak root chakra could result in a weakened metabolism and immune system resulting from a compromised working of the adrenal glands which are responsible for releasing and producing chemical messengers needed for all the physiological, chemical and biological functions of your body.

A not-so-strong root chakra results in nervousness and a sense of insecurity whereas an overly working root chakra could result in greed and a sense of excessive materialism.

Sacral Chakra – Governs the reproductive glands which are the ovaries (for the females) and the testes (for the males. The well-balanced and healthy root chakra facilitates the uninterrupted functioning of these glands ensuring well-developed sexuality in the person.

The root chakra also regulates the production and secretion of the sex hormones. The potential for life formation in the ovaries is reflected in the sacral chakra as these two energies are connected.

When this chakra is open and free, you are able to express your sexuality well without being overly emotional. You feel a comforting sense of intimacy with your partner. A healthy sacral chakra enhances your passion and liveliness and helps you manage your sexuality without feeling burdened with undue emotions.

A sacral chakra that is not functioning at its peak efficiency is bound to leave you frigid, very close to people and relationships, and poker-faced. On the contrary, a weak sacral chakra will make you feel overly and unnecessarily, emotionally compelling you to attach yourself to people for a sense of security and belonging. Your feelings could be overly sexual towards one and all.

Solar Plexus Chakra – This controls the pancreas, which is directly connected to the sugar (through the control of insulin secretion) and, therefore, energy levels in your body. Thus, if this chakra is not working properly you could potentially have a weak pancreas, resulting in a compromised metabolic state. Compromised pancreas could lead to digestive problems, lowered blood sugar levels, ulcers, poor memory, etc. which are all connected with a bad metabolism.

Heart Chakra – Regulates the thymus gland and through it, the entire immune system. Being the center of love, compassion, spirituality, and group consciousness, a malfunctioning heart chakra will result in the malfunctioning of the thymus gland leaving you prone to low immunity.

Our feelings and thoughts towards ourselves play a crucial role in keeping our immune system working well. When we love ourselves our immune system is powerful and strong. When we are uncertain of ourselves and our strengths and our capabilities, we feel disappointed which drives us to react wrongly to negative things.

All these negativities leave our immune system weak and we end up holding on to toxins. It is imperative to keep our heart chakra healthy by investing time and energy in self-love so that our immune system is strengthened. An underactive heart chakra makes you feel distant and cold and an overactive one could result in selfish love in your heart. Be wary of both states and work at keeping your chakra balanced.

Throat Chakra – controls and regulates the thyroid gland and hence is directly responsible for a healthy metabolism and to regulate body temperature. This is the center of communication and plays a vital role in the way you speak, write, or think. An unbalanced throat chakra results in a malfunctioning thyroid resulting in an overall poor physical, mental, and emotional health.

Third Eye Chakra – directly controls the functioning of the pituitary gland or the master gland which controls and regulates other organs and glands in the human body. The Pineal gland is many times associated with this chakra too, as we already know that a well-coordinated, combined working of the pineal and the pituitary glands is responsible to keep our entire body, mind, and spirit well-oiled and working well.

Crown Chakra – This regulates the functioning of the pineal gland, which controls our biological cycle and our circadian rhythm.

Chakras And Their Origins

The spiritual communities in the west are greatly influenced by Catholicism and Christianity, but there are many other religious and spiritual ideas that mix and meld in the west, especially in the United States. Many of these spiritual communities accept practices like yoga and meditation but leave the philosophical topics as their own. Focusing on these powerful physical practices, these spiritual communities miss to adopt the symbolism and myth, which is left abandoned. Chakras seem to be permeating this barrier with the ideas held true by many people in Indian and the Far East.

Chakras are welcomed by many spiritual adherents who find the ideas helpful in grasping the relationship between the physical and the spiritual. We see Christianity and chakras working together most prominently in New Age communities as they mix and match practices from many cultures to create their young spiritual communities. The New Age movement may be known for an abundance of frauds and false teachers, but it has still played a great role in introducing eastern concepts with western conservative beliefs. Chakras are a great example of this.

The concept of chakras can be viewed in two ways: They can be seen as a symbolic way to organize our life experiences and examine them, or, on the other hand, they can be viewed as actual energetic centers that bridge the gap between the physical and spiritual bodies. As we explore these concepts, remember to keep an open mind. For our intents and purposes with this book, we will adhere to the idea that chakras are both of these views. They are great symbolism, but also they are actual energetic centers that can be personally worked with.

The ancient concept of chakras recognizes that chakras are energetic centers found in our subtle spiritual body. This is a further disambiguation of the concept that we all have of our physical bodies that are twinned by a subtle energetic or spiritual body. Chakras act as a means in which our physical bodies interact and influence our spiritual bodies.

Many communities in the modern age have accepted that energy is key to understanding our life experiences. Science has proven that humans are electromagnetic in nature, and this energy moves and adapts to changes in our emotional state or environment. These scientific breakthroughs are related to chakras as a means to physically feel the energy we give off or that others give off. Consider anytime you've gotten a bad vibe from someplace or someone.

The subtle energetic body needs to be cared for just as our physical body does. This is where chakra work comes into play. It is thought that chakras get blocked or closed, and we can actively work with these blockages, helping to maintain their health and consistent flow of energy between the physical and the spiritual worlds. Most traditions consider a certain chakra to be associated with a certain aspect of life, each chakra having different governance over its attributed aspects.

It is thought that there are over 80,000 different chakras throughout our bodies, claiming influence over the most subtle experiences, even experiences that we can't even feel or recognize. Most traditions do not see it worthwhile to work directly with individual chakras that are small or minuscule; so many texts are only focused on a handful of more important chakras. The main chakras are usually numbered between four and seven, respectively. With the complexity of human experience, it only makes sense that there are thousands of subtle energetic centers surrounding our bodies, not unlike the thousands of subtle autonomous occurrences that transpire in our body every moment that we physically feel.

The main chakras are much easier to notice, having a greater impact on our day-to-day lives and aspects that we constantly pay attention to. The main chakra model found in the west is the seven chakra model. These seven main chakras are recognized as the most important energetic centers in most contemporary traditions. These seven chakras are thought to encompass all aspects of our lives, from emotional experience, physical ailments, and spiritual awareness. Depending on how healthy our chakras are, these experiences can be favorable or detrimental, and in turn, affect the chakras as well, creating a cycle of energetic flow that influences our lives in incredible ways.

There may be thousands of small minuscule chakras, but these energy centers are more difficult to work with than the larger more influential chakras, that are recognized by spiritual communities and some scientific communities alike. It is worth mentioning, that it has been shown that many of the energetic pathways that our far away ancestors adhered to, actually match the nerve pathways throughout our bodies.

The ancient cultures that worked with chakras fully believed that humans lived simultaneously in the physical world and the subtle energetic world. The physical is more easy to study than the metaphysical or energetic. In fact, the physical can be observed and studied in a laboratory setting. On the other hand, the energetic world is much more abstract and unpredictable. Some people look at the physical as the only component of life. This approach is way too simplistic to encompass all of our experiences, including consciousness, perception, and other phenomena which cannot be explained or proven by science.

The main chakras will be our point of focus in this book, just as it was for our oldest ancestors. We will work to master the practices that allow us to interact directly with the chakras, thus altering our lives for the better.

We will see how these essential bridges between the physical and the spiritual world can sometimes get blocked or closed. The reasons can be different; it can be due to emotional problems, mental unbalance, and even physical ailments. Through the techniques in this book, we will learn to help our chakras stay healthy and flowing consistently.

We have now loosely defined what the chakras are, but we need to continue exploring the history and meaning of these incredible energy centers. Getting to know as much as we can about the history of chakras will help us better understand how the concepts have evolved into what they are today, how they work, and how to work with them. Simply finding the most recent source of chakras information could very well be flawed in many ways. By learning the etymology and history of these concepts, we can develop a personal practice that suits our needs, and develop our own personal views and opinions on these ancient concepts. How everyone else thinks about chakras may not fit into your perception, and of course,

certain practices that work for others may not work for you. You need to develop a relationship with chakras that is personal to yourself, letting some (if not all) the practices we will discuss in this book transform your life for the better. This personalization will go a long way to further your practice and let it grow to reach your desired goals.

Etymology

Before directing towards the more practical part of the book, it is worth spending a few words on the etymology behind the concept of chakras.

The word chakra itself can be translated loosely to mean 'wheel'. This is because of the circular shape of chakras and the idea that they spin when opened or healthy. Many believe that when the chakras are closed or blocked, they do not spin at all or will spin in the opposite direction. These wheels need our attention and support to remain open and operating. This will allow the subtle energetic aspects of our lives to influence our physical ones. Such a symbiotic relationship is key in most eastern traditions and is very popular in India. These cultures heavily rely on the concept of chakras to organize and prioritize their lives, not to mention to access a world of healing outside of the modern medical sphere.

Chakras are attributed to certain physiological conditions that many humans face. Hormone production, nervous system ailments, organ health, and more generally, any other condition can be attributed to a certain chakra. Therefore, if someone is experiencing a problem in the physical world, working with the attributed chakra could help to fix the issue on a metaphysical level. Essentially, this is energy work: by healing ourselves energetically, we can heal ourselves physically.

This is not all. There are other attributes to chakras outside of the medical sphere as well. Each chakra contains many attributes associated with the physical world and our experiences as humans. Seed syllables are assigned to chakras, and these are ancient primal sounds used for mantras or meditation. Each chakra also has a color attribute, and if a chakra is blocked, the attributed color will help to open it, and keep the energy flowing. There are musical keys related to chakras, each one helping its attributed chakra by being exposed to the sound. Stones, herbs, symbols, organs, but also illnesses are all associated with a certain chakra as their energetic center. These attributes can be viewed as symbolic or actual attributes of the chakras.

On a symbolical level, we can work with the chakras through meditation to heal our minds. On a physical level, the chakras will open when aligned with the above mentioned attributes.

These interactions work on many levels and are hard to pinpoint with scientific analysis. However, either way, these practices work and can and should be utilized in our day to day lives.

It is safe to say that any interaction you have in your daily life affects your chakras in either a positive or negative way. This is where mindfulness will come into play. We need to navigate our lives in the most efficient manner to lead a fulfilling and enjoyable existence. By being aware of our surroundings and our choices, we can find our way through the world with ease. Chakras can lead us to achieve this by helping us organize our experiences and make mindful decisions each and every day. By taking the time to analyze all of our decisions through a "chakra lens", we can find paths through our chaotic world that we may not otherwise see.

Cultural Uses

Much of what we know about chakras in the west is predominantly influenced by Hinduism and Buddhist thought. These philosophies are very popular in these cultures and are used throughout the variety of religions and spiritual practices. There are also many other cultures that adhere to the idea of a spiritual body interacting simultaneously with our physical world. As an example, in Traditional Chinese Medicine, we find acupuncture and acupressure, which adhere to the concepts that there are energetic lay lines throughout the body that can be worked with.

Other cultures also adhere to the idea of an energetic presence. Almost every ancient culture owns in one form or the other the idea of the existence of a connecting energetic web. A form of energy which links all living things and beings, and which is also how we interact with the world in the nonphysical. In this book, we will center our focus on the eastern philosophies, mainly on the Indian influence and culture. As above-mentioned, the concept of chakras does not require any religion, but these concepts do stem from religious cultures. Hence, we must familiarize ourselves with their origins to be able to approach these ideas with respect and humility.

Chakra Working Basics

As we continue our exploration of the origins of chakras, we need to also touch on the very basics of how the chakra practices work. These practices vary from culture to culture. Many cultures believe that we must turn on our chakras to begin working with them. This is often symbolized as a dormant energy at the base of the spine that needs to be awakened. This dormant energy is known as Kundalini, the serpent, or snake, that guides energy up down the spine.

To awake these energies, we must be balanced both physically and energetically. The chakra energy is very concentrated and needs to be approached with patience and an open mind. Even the slightest bit of work with chakras can cause dramatic changes, this is known as a Kundalini awakening and it is not recommended that we awaken this energy in any other way except with a balanced practice and hard work.

Short cuts and use of drugs for these reasons almost always have detrimental repercussions. Opening the chakras takes dedication and determination. Depending on how blocked your chakras are, it could even take years to get the energy flowing. On the other hand, this is not a written rule, some people have documented their personal experience, with their chakras being opened in only a matter of weeks.

Despite the growing attention towards the concept of chakras and the rise in popularity, still today, the nature of chakras has yet to be fully understood, parts of it still remaining in mystery.

These energy centers truly are unique to each individual, and it is up to us to develop our own personal practice and determine what goals we are trying to reach through this practice. We have learned what chakras are and how they work, but what about their history and variety of practice from one culture to another?

The concept of chakras can be dated back to the first use of the word, but the ideas most certainly predate the written word. Even if they were yet to be called chakras, these concepts have existed in many cultures throughout history. These energetic models of reality and the true nature of the unseen forces that we interact with is at the core of every spiritual practice.

The actual use of the word chakra is first found in the Vedas, one of the most important texts in the Hindu culture. Many religions and spiritual models have sprung from these ancient texts, some using chakras some that do not. The way we define chakras today was not found in these texts. Chakras were used more like an intensive visualization tool that had a more mysterious origin than we know today.

The Vedas contained and invaluable expanse of esoteric knowledge that has now touched almost every popular religion we know. They were defined as the "king that turns the wheel of the empire", moving in every direction from a center point. We see here the related symbolism of the chakra wheels. There is also the idea of the Vedic fire altar, where there are five symbols used for visualization. These symbols were the triangle, square, circle, crescent moon, and dumpling. These shapes are also used today for chakra visualization and mandalas.

The concept of the dormant energy at the base of the spine is found in the Vedas as well, namely the Rigveda. This story tells of a yogi named Kunamnama, which is literally translated as "she who is coiled". This energy is known today as Kundalini, but the story of Kunamnama is the earliest reference to the dormant serpent energy at the base of every human's spine. This energy is known to travel the spine from its base to the base of the skull. It travels along a pathway known as Nadis.

These concepts are first found in the Upanishads form the 1st millennium BCE. Here we see the appearance of the modern chakra system, even if, for the most part we see only four main chakras with these older systems, as compared to the seven found in contemporary times. It is difficult to pin down the exact origins of the seven chakra model, but it is safe to assume that it progressively formed as the different chakra systems traveled throughout the east and made its way west, adopting new ideas and evolving into what we know it as today.

Energy models like the ones to which we adhere to today can be found since the 8th century, in Buddhist texts. These texts included chakra concepts, some earlier texts referencing vortexes that were energetic nature, although the texts do not explore them in detail. Prana and Nadi are also found during this era but lack exact origin in the texts. These words have become powerful and common in our current society with or without exact historical context, as if they have minds of their own, moving throughout the timeline right into modern times.

Buddhist texts seem to have the most influential documentation of the chakra model as we know it. Certainly, there are precursors to these texts, but the Buddhist practices concentrated heavily on these ideas, giving way to the practices we know today. The Buddhists found that there are four main chakras, these were named as Manipura, Anahata, Vishuddha and Ushnisha. These names can be loosely translated into English as Navel, heart, throat, and crown. This was often seen as spiritual counterparts to our human experiences and emotions, or the physical self twinned by the energetic or spiritual self. These ideas sparked many varying sects of Buddhist thought be split off into a variety of traditions, many that are still teaching today.

One the tradition, the Tibetan sect of Buddhism, takes the chakra models and uses the ideas of Prana and Nadis as a means to balance one's life. At the core of Tibetan Buddhism, there is the idea that learning to control the Prana through breath work, manipulating it to move through the Nadis, was the central most important practice used to reach unity with the universe. This is akin to the Kundalini energy found in Hinduism, as both models aim to reach an enlightened state through the use of energetic centers in and around our bodies.

Hindu tantric traditions are more closely related to the modern system of chakras. These traditions adhere to the Seven Chakra System, mainly inspired by hatha yoga. There are many differing views on the chakra tradition within Hinduism, but the Seven Chakra System if the most prominent and obviously the main tradition that made its way to the west.

The chakra models in Hinduism developed alongside the popular religion of Shaktism. Shakti is the premiere goddess in Hindu and other Indian traditions. The kundalini energy is even attributed to Shakti in many traditions. The chakras as energy centers are found in this system, with almost any Shakti based system adhering to the Seven Chakra System.

Death

When it comes to death within these systems, we need to consider the idea of reincarnation as the most widely practiced belief system.

The idea that death is not the end of life itself, but a transgression into many other worlds. It is thought that the soul or spirit of someone may travel extensively before returning to Earth if they return at all.

In the chakra system if a person dies, their energy would leave the body behind, traveling without the body's restraints. There are a number of places this energy may travel. Many believe it returns to a source, then may leave there as well. This is similar to the idea of what this energy does when we sleep as well. Many eastern traditions believe that when we sleep, our energy is turned inward, traveling through dream-like realms. We catch glimpses of these journeys in dreams or astral projection practices.

This gives rise to questions of the physical body versus the spiritual. Many people may believe that our physical bodies are not important and that we should focus mostly on our spirit progress. In reality, while we are living with our physical bodies, we need to take great care for them as well. The physical and the energetic exist as one as far as the earthly experience is concerned. We need to care for our entire being, as we know it, to achieve our desired results.

The many chakra systems that are found throughout history are interrelated in many complex ways. It is obvious that these concepts have borrowed from each other, melding together to form the systems we know today, including the Seven Chakra System that is so popular in the west. These systems have been at the core of many eastern traditions, and as the west accepts this ancient knowledge even more of the population begins to work with these systems, mixing them with their own practices and creating the chakra systems we know today.

Chapter 6 Chakras Massages

There are various massage techniques that people can use to improve their focus and connect with their chakras. There are several massage techniques you can try, such as:

Deep-Tissue Massage

Practicing this form of massage on your back is the first step you should take. The deep-tissue practice is not necessarily deep but rather slow and specific to a particular part. The main goal is to massage a particular muscle in a focused and slow manner using a broadening stroke or lengthening stroke meaning with or across the fiber, respectively.

When performing deep-tissue massage, the biggest advantage is focusing on the fascia or connective tissue. According to research, the connective tissue is the wiring of the energy flow in the human body. The fascia, on the other hand, acts as the conduit through which the energy in our body flows. This will enable us to focus on the erector spinae muscles with the determination to work with prana or chakra energy.

Practice lengthening strokes on your iliocostalis, longissimus, and the spinalis. Also, practice broadening strokes on the gluteus media, which will enable you to open the flow of the energy that connects prana with the legs. Also, practice broadening stroke on the longissimus.

Reflexology

Another technique is the "chakra" foot reflexology massage. The reflexology practice focuses on two chakra aspects: Chakra's physical location and the endocrine gland that is associated with each chakra either through close proximity or related function. The physical locations are situated along with the head reflex points on your feet and along the spinal as well.

The root chakra is located at the sacrum, and the root chakra reflex in your foot is in the sacral reflex on your foot. The seventh chakra reflex is found on the big toe's distal portion. The chakras are associated with the main endocrine glands.

All the other chakras are positioned in the feet as well. Also, there are other places that connect to the chakras such as sciatic nerve which connect with the root chakra, uterus connects to the sacral chakra, and the solar plexus and heart reflex connect to the third chakra and fourth chakra respectively.

Energy Work

Another technique is the chakra energy work. The light touch is the focus of the energy work over chakra while also focusing on the intended purpose. Focus on the connection and intention as well. Focus your visualization on two aspects, including working with the right (visual, intuitive) and left (analytic, logical) sides of your brain. Visualize colored energy in a spinning wheel on each part of the chakra (on the right brain).

Life Energy Massage

It is one of the most popular techniques. The main focus of life energy massage session is the advanced healing energy to clear the body. The cleansing involves getting rid of old feelings or habitual thought patterns. The session will enable you to clear negative thinking, clear past traumas, expansive feelings, improved sleep, increase energy, etc.

It's a gentle hand-on kind of session.

Chakra Foot Massage

In this form of chakra massage therapy, start by preparing a tub, foot bath, a small basin or a large bowl here bot your feet can fit comfortably. Lay a towel beside you to set and dry your legs and protect your floor. Add several teaspoons of sea or Epsom salt (you can also use coarse sea salt which is readily available in many grocery stores). Fill the very hot water, but it should not be too hot to hurt burn your legs. You can wait for the water to get cold for a few minutes.

You can also add few drops of recommended essential oil and an oil blend, perform massage on both feet, one at a time. When you are done with massaging one foot, put it in water as you massage the second one. After massaging both feet, place them in water and let them stay there for 10 to 15 minutes as long as the water is still hot. That's why it is still important to prepare very hot water. Breathe in and exhale smoothly. You can perform this form of meditation while listening to cool music; the use of chakra affirmations is also great. You can also prepare an inspiring statement that you can be reading while practicing this meditation.

For instance, if you are practicing root chakra, you can say, "I am grounded, I am safe, and the process of life is trustworthy."

You can also use the color that represents the chakra you are trying to heal. For your root chakra, use a red towel or blanket and so on for the rest of the chakras.

The main difference between getting a chakra massage and other types of massages like the regular massage is the knowledge about the chakra locations by chakra professionals massage providers. The expert giving you chakra massages will be able to facilitate your body's connection with your wisdom. They will be able to connect with you as a client or their patient properly, their main focus will be to balance or heal your chakra, they will be able to align the healing process with your intentions for concrete solutions. They will prepare the room and make sure it's warm and has a receptive environment to enable the quality meditation process and effective healing.

How Different Chakras Can Be Healed Or Balanced Through Massage Therapy

Root chakra: With this chakra regarded as the foundation of the whole chakra system, it's good health is required just like the rest of the chakras. A professional chakra massage therapist will recommend the stimulation of your back through reflexology and balancing massage.

Solar Plexus: Located above the navel and below the heart, it is also regarded as the power center. Our power center can experience imbalance in situations such as the transition from adolescence to adulthood, dealing with a job loss or transition of your career. A professional chakra therapist will recommend deep-tissue massage in your back to realign the chakras.

Throat Chakra: This chakra is represented in throat and neck areas. A chakra massage expert will not just master the massage practice and perform it on you but will also master the communication practice as well. They will help with massaging your neck and throat areas to help you have a relaxing and comfortable expression and communication.

Crown Chakra: This is a chakra that helps connect with the higher purpose and relate to your wisdom. When this chakra is in good condition, you will are able to enjoy the full joy of our universe and feel blissful. The use of aromatherapy and deep-tissue massage will greatly in giving you this desirable feeling.

Use Of Clockwise Circular Stroke

You can also practice this form of massage using water medicated and soluble oils alongside with the herbs. The root chakra can be massaged on the coccyx using dashmoola oil, which is formed from a blend of 10 herbs. The sacral chakra regulates creativity, sexual functions, and water balance. Dilute essential oil used for sacral chakra and massage the sacrum or the lower abdomen. For solar plexus, massage the navel area with ginger oils and peppermint.

The heart chakra is massaged at the upper back and the center of the chest using diluted basil oil. The throat chakra is massaged on the throat using oil that is infused with calamus. The third eye can be massaged with triphala or oil infused with a rose at the center of your forehead. The crown chakra is massaged at its chakra point as well, which is at the top of the head.

Massage therapies are excellent solution when looking for a way to balance and heal your chakras. In most cases, when one chakra is not allowing energy to flow freely either because of imbalance or blockage, massages will be of great help. Massages are applied to the correct places and will help you restore their correct energy. It is also easy to correct your chakra, especially if you are new and trying to heal or balance the chakra because you will identify with exact chakra points and master their locations. It is also advisable for you to combine massages with other practices such as health and the right diet, exercise, and meditation.

When there is a smooth flow of energies through your chakras, you will have stable and balanced mental, physical, emotional, and spiritual health. Chakra massage therapy is an excellent technique which does not only help you realign your chakras but also make you feel better, relax, and rejuvenated after the chakra massage sessions.

Chapter 7 Connecting to your heart energy

Connecting to your heart energy will have a huge impact on your healing journey and will help you maintain an equilibrium of "everything will be okay and I am good at taking care of my needs". Once you get going with chakra healing work, you open up a whole lot of different kinds of cans of worms that need to be addressed and understood. This can be an emotional time and you may feel inclined to reject a lot of your feelings or experiences and can end up reverting back to old habits and patterns that feel more "comfortable".

The truth is, your only comfortable in those realities because you had to teach yourself to live that way (ex: always avoiding confrontation at the expense of your own feelings; choosing the bottle of red wine over water and a good night's sleep; telling yourself you will never get that promotion, over and over again). As much as you have learned how to live your life with certain behaviors, thoughts and ideas, you can unlearn them by teaching yourself new ways to balance and harmonize your energy to reflect more of your true nature.

What is true nature and how do you find that out? If you are ever struggling and fighting against yourself (and even others: projection), you will be acting against what you are truly wanting for yourself. If you are working in a career that drains your energy and makes you feel unhappy, then you are not in the right career for yourself. If you are uncomfortable staying married to someone who causes you to doubt how you like to be, then you are likely not in the right relationship for you. If you are struggling to stay focused on what it is that you are truly wanting to do with your life, it is because you are listening to your fears that it won't be possible.

Finding balance and harmony with yourself means that you have to work everyday to understand what your attitude toward your life and yourself is, and how to maintain that philosophy and energy. Through the healing process of working with your chakras, you will uncover so much of these truths about who you are, what you want the most, and what is likely standing in your path to getting there.

Finding harmony and balance in those times can feel like a chore and your energy and attitude to your growth is what will help you continue moving forward. The best ways to achieve harmony and balance are to work with the energy of opposites. Here is an example of what that means:

- You are angry and frustrated and can't seem to smooth your feathers after weeks of feeling stuck in a rut with your chakra healing practices. You are engaging with all of the methods that were shown to you and you still have made any breakthroughs. You feel unsure of what to do next and so you allow yourself to feel painful and uneasy about what you are doing, rejecting the goals you had in mind, and the process you are going through.

- To regain harmony and balance, consider the energy that you are holding onto. It is saying that you can't do this and that you will never figure out how to heal like this, or that you should just quit because you can't see any big differences or changes. If you have these feelings come up, they are asking you to shift your ideas and look for alternative voice inside of yourself to inform your progress. The harmony and balance that you can regain comes from teaching yourself how to effectively process this type of feeling.

- To reassure yourself that you are doing well, you can alter your perception of the situation by contemplating your emotions and why they are happening in the first place. Did you have an immediate result in mind? Do you plan on your healing only taking a certain amount of time? Are you eager to change and therefore frustrated because you have noticed any major shifts? Are you able to recognize that the very feelings you are having pertain to growth and that you are making progress, right in this moment?

- Harmony and balance require reflection and contemplation. To achieve this state of being, you have to question your position, your feelings, your experiences.

It may seem too simple, but the truth is, you will always fluctuate back and forth until you have learned how to understand you own energetic processes. When something is feeling negative, look for how it is positive (opposites). It isn't hard to find the patterns, once you really begin to pay attention. Once you identify the patterns you create with your emotions and energies, then you will know how to change them, thus regaining balance and harmony.

Be patient with yourself and act from a curiosity rather than a judgement of yourself. You can always find better inner harmony when you are inquisitive instead of accusatory.

Applications for Everyday

Your everyday chakra healing practice is already all laid out for you in this book. Each chapter has given you all of the knowledge, understanding and tools you need to begin this momentous journey. There are places for you to dig deeply into yourself and uncover your beautiful truths, buried underneath the layers of energetic blockages and imbalances. What is lurking under there? Are you ready to look?

To help you give focus to your healing path with your chakras, here is a list of everyday applications to keep you in focus and practice:

1. Begin your day with a meditation and some yoga instead of 3 cups of coffee.

2. Spend time in the morning sun with your journal and time for reflection.

3. Practice mindfulness on your way to work.

4. Take a meditation break at the office.

5. Carry your preferred chakra healing crystals with you so you can feel energetically harmonious.

6. Take time in your day to check in with your feelings and your physical body. As yourself if you have tension anywhere, or what kinds of thoughts are you focusing on?

7. Visit a place that has meaning for you.

8. Practice a self-love meditation.

9. At the end of your day, determine where you are feeling the most "off" and perform a chakra healing meditation to get you back in balance.

10. Eat a healthy meal and have a relaxing evening with friends and/or family.

11. Get a good night's sleep.

12. Take good care of your body by listening to it when it is shouting out to you that something is off.

13. Enjoy some indulgences every once and a while.

14. Find a moment in your day to dance or sing.

15. Share your feelings with a friend, colleague or partner.

16. Offer yourself time to do something creative.

17. Do something you have been afraid to try.

18. Spend time in nature.

19. Spend time in water (baths, swimming, etc.)

20. Devote time to yourself alone.

21. Record your experiences and keep a diary of your progress.

22. Listen to your words as they come up for acknowledgement in your mind and discover what your mind is telling you; where does it lead (which chakra)?

There are so many ways to look for healing and opening in your energy centers. These applications are only the beginning of how to start helping your energy shift every day. The more you practice understanding your energy, the easier it becomes to listen and respond to what you are really needing, wanting, and asking to remove and rebalance. Look for ways to enjoy these applications in your own life, or find some that are not listed here that really work for you. Your journey is in your hands and your energy is ready to vibrate at a higher frequency. Practice self-love, bring balance and harmony back into your life, and do it every day!

Chapter 8 The Benefits Of Reiki

The many benefits of Reiki healing is the main reason why many people choose this particular form of touch therapy over others. Reiki is a dormant healing ability within everyone but since it has rarely been used, most people are unable to harness its true power and its life changing benefits. But, like anything, the more we practice something the better and more proficient we become at it. Another thing that makes Reiki such an effective form of healing is that it encourages us to take responsibility for our own health instead of solely relying on doctors and medicines. It puts the power into our own hands, metaphorically and literally.

Since Reiki works on a vibrational level with the body's energy centers and on the aural plane, it can have a profound healing effect on the whole person. This works because the energy is naturally sent where it needs to go in the body. This energy has an intelligence of its own and can read where exactly to travel in the body. If the patient requires psychological healing it will travel towards the higher chakras such as the crown and the third eye. If suffering from an illness, the energy will most likely travel to the thymus where the immune system resides, in order to give it a boost.

In both hands-on healing and distance healing sessions, it is important to not only consent to the healing energy of Reiki being sent but to actively accept and welcome the energy into our bodies.

Visualize it working and feel its presence. By accepting this power of Reiki, we allow the energy to flow where it needs to.

Some of the many reported physical include:

- Deeper level of relaxation.

- Relief from physical pain and reduced intensity of chronic pain.

- Physical healing of illness or injury.

- Increased immune function which improves the body's ability to heal.

- Relief from common aches and pains such as muscle and joint pain, headache and stomach aches.

- Relief from muscle tension.

- Promotion of a positive mindset and healthy body.

- Increased energy levels.

- Better sleep patterns and the ability to sleep longer and more soundly.

- Reduced blood pressure.

- More efficient removal of toxins from the body.

- Compliments other forms of treatment and therapy including clinical and contemporary forms of medicine.

- Relief from and reduced episodes of asthma.

- Healing and clearing a variety of skin conditions.

- Improved resistance to viruses such as colds and flu.

- Reduced pain and discomfort from ulcers.

- Relief from and reduced pain and discomfort caused by arthritis or back pain by improving joint mobility and movement.

As you can see, the physical benefits of Reiki are numerous and can impact a wide range of conditions. No matter who you are or what you are suffering from, Reiki helps to heal, clear, reduce and improve physical well-being.

HEALING THE PHYSICAL BODY

The physical benefits of healing the body with Reiki is often the main reason many people seek out this powerful form of therapy. Some of the physical benefits Reiki has been linked to include its ability to lower blood pressure and heart rate, positively impact hormone levels, increase endorphins, boost the immune system and can also be used in combination with medical treatments. This strengthens our ability to fully recover. Here is a quick recap and some of the reasons Reiki has become so popular today.

- It is a therapy that is available to everyone regardless of age, gender, background, income or medical history.

- It can be practiced by anyone with or without professional training.

- It is gentle and non-invasive – all you need to do is lay down, relax and consciously allow the healing to occur. This is a big advantage particularly if us or the patient are injured or in pain.

- It is natural. No use of special equipment or external medicines, therefore no chances of side effects. It works directly with universal energy, the energy of the practitioner and your own life force energy.

- It links into your chakras/energy centers, healing and clearing blockages and imbalances by disrupting the flow of negative energy that creates disease and illness.

BOOST THE IMMUNE SYSTEM WITH REIKI

A method of self-healing to boost the immune system will be described next. Like the first exercise we must first get ourselves into a quiet and comfortable place. Now please follow the guidelines provided.

 *Cho Ku Rei*

1. Begin by focusing on the power symbol cho ku rei. Visualize or draw it in the air in front of you.

2. Place one hand over the thymus area (upper central chest) with the opposite hand covering the solar plexus.

3. Once in this position, bring your focus to the thymus gland area.

4. In your mind, imagine the Power symbol a few feet out in front of you, in line with the thymus.

5. Visualize the Power symbol in the thymus, within your body.

6. Now also see the Power symbol a few feet behind you. Again, in line with the thymus.

7. At this point you should be seeing three symbols. One in front, one inside and one behind. All in line of the thymus area.

8. Inhale deeply and visualize bringing in Reiki life force energy in with your breath.

9. Imagine a beam of light from the Symbol in front of you, passing through your body to the symbol behind you. You should envision a rod of light energy passing through you at your thymus area while you continue breathing deeply.

10. Continue to breathe deeply. While visualizing an energy source moving out in front of you and then behind you through this beam effect. It should

look like a ball of energy, moving backwards and forwards.

11. It should take the ball of energy, a second or two to move from the front to the back and so on. Control the speed of the energy ball with your breath.

12. Continue this for a few minutes. Once you feel ready to come out of this process. Slowly start to clear your mind. Imagine closing up any chakras which may have been opened during this exercise.

13. Finally seal the energy as was discussed earlier. Pull a imaginary zipper up from the bottom of your feet to the top of your head.

14. Your healing is complete.

This is a very powerful technique for boosting the immune system and with regular practice the ability to recover from minor illnesses becomes much easier. It is a form of a healing meditation using the power of Reiki energy.

Chapter 9 The Magic of Meditation

The Rich History, the Overall Mindset and More

Ah, yes! This chapter is going to be one I am sure you are excited to read. But not nearly as excited as I am to write it! I love giving practical exercises and examples for you so that you can further your education in a more realistic way. After all, I can tell you all about meditation and chakras until I am blue in the face (or fingers). That does nothing to help you move forward towards serenity and enlightenment, however.

So, what is meditation, exactly? I know that you must have heard of it. This is a highly popularized activity that most people have a very strong opinion on. It is seen as tedious at best and, at worst, totally unnecessary.

Of course, those who deem it unnecessary or unhelpful are entirely ignorant of the topic.

I want to give you a full rundown on meditation here. I am going to go over the general history, including the geographical origin of meditation. On top of this, I will give you multiple types of meditation you can practice and the benefits of them.

There is, even more, I will be going over... but you will just have to keep reading in order to find out what is in store for you!

The type of meditation we are going to explore was originally developed in India. I am sure there is no surprise there since that seems to be the origin point for most topics in this book. There are many pieces of ancient wall art that show the use of meditation being used as far back as 5,000 BCE. This shows that meditation grew and formed at least simultaneously to Buddhism. The truth is, however, that the two probably share the same origin and simply split as time moved forward.

The practice of meditation can be seen all over the globe. However, we cannot forget its roots in eastern philosophy- more specifically, India.

It is not just Buddhists who took to the idea of meditation, however. You will see many other eastern philosophies and religions drawing from the power offered by meditation. Taoism, which is a religion originating in China, is a prime example of this. Each of these eastern philosophies has generally developed its own form of meditation or several different forms. The best part about meditation is that there are so many different types out there that it makes it easy to find one you truly mesh with.

Do not be mistaken, however. There is definitely scholarly proof that meditation also took hold in the west. This is mainly due to the obvious power inherent in meditative practices. Practicing mindfulness is one of the best ways to encourage your overall happiness and feelings of internal serenity.

The word meditation actually comes from the French word

"meditacioun", rather than Sanskrit. This, in turn, comes from the Latin word "meditatio", which translates roughly to "to think or reflect upon".

However, the Buddha was, of course, a huge proponent of meditation. In fact, this is one of the practices that brings you to a state of enlightenment. This is why clearing your chakras through meditation is crucial for your path to inner, and outer peace. Making sure that you understand the world around you as it truly is will also play a crucial role, and is another area in which meditation, and mindfulness, help you. As you can imagine, conducting yourself in an ethical manner is the last of these three.

There are several uses for meditation, and the benefits are too many to name. I will do my best to make sure you understand almost every benefit there is, nonetheless, I want you to have a full comprehension of the power that meditation can provide. Cleaning your chakras properly requires the usage of meditation… and the proper usage, at that. Have no fear on that end, however. I will be going over everything you need in the way of exercises.

First, let me go over the major benefits you can gain from daily meditation.

- Enhancing self-awareness: The path to enlightenment begins with self-reflection or spending some time at peace with the world. As you begin to explore the inner realms of yourself, you will begin to cultivate self-awareness. This is something everybody could stand to gain. There is a growing problem with a lack of self-awareness, mainly due to the modern technology available.

Spending some time away from everything locked in a meditative state will always bring you a better overall awareness.

- Generate external kindness: Making sure you do right by others is not just a constituent of Buddhism. It is also a tenant of constituent human decency. Participating in daily meditation is proven to help people practice kindness towards others. There is something about the inner peace that pushes you to provide others with the same peace of mind.

- Regulates emotional health: When you feel as though your emotions are out of control, turning to meditation can be a healthy way to deal with it. Regulating your emotions will come easier and easier as you explore the depths of meditation. Emotional balance is the cornerstone of inner peace and a better life overall.

- Grants better concentration: If you have trouble with concentration, meditation has an answer for that. It has been shown scientifically that experiencing the clarity that meditation is so known for will often bring you

- better concentration overall. It tells your brain to slow down and think more rationally about things.

- Builds mental connections: Speaking of which, meditation has also been shown to help build new connections in the brain. Since you are entering a state of mindfulness, it is almost like being "asleep" while you are awake. When you sleep, you are building connections in your brain. You can trick your brain into thinking you are sleeping by slowing down your body and entering true mindfulness.

- Keeps anxiety levels low: This goes hand in hand with the idea of emotional regulation. Even beyond this, however, is the pursuit of lowering anxiety levels. For some, this is a serious disorder that requires treatment. Most therapists will strongly suggest picking up mindfulness or meditation to help cope.

In fact, it is a crucial part of one of the most popular, and successful, treatment methods currently available. This treatment is called "Cognitive Behavioral Therapy" if you were curious!

- Allows for better stress management: Overall stress is a huge contributor to people being unhappy and overwhelmed. Bringing your stress levels down is crucial to living a happy, full life. Meditation gives you the opportunity to put your worries, fears, and anger aside for a few minutes. This gives you the chance to cool down and think about things more rationally afterward.

Remember that the list of benefits is exhaustive and could go on forever. These are just a few of the ways I think meditation benefits common people in their day-to-day lives. You will also notice that while we talk about meditation I will step further away from Buddhism on the whole. While this is a crucial thing to understand on your road to understanding chakras, I want it to be also appealing to anybody who may be reading this.

The truth is that you do not have to practice Buddhism to meditate or practice mindfulness. You will be doing so on "accident", but consciously doing so is not necessarily required.

Chapter 10 Every Day Practices

You now know how to start your own mindfulness meditation practice, but you might be wondering how you can bring mindfulness into your everyday life. You also may not be interested in adopting a meditation routine, but you can still bring mindfulness into your life with a few simple actions.

As you have learned, humans have a tendency to go on autopilot, and this happens more often during the normal everyday tasks we have to do. These are the moments when you need to become more mindful. You don't have to clear your mind of everything, just become aware of what you are doing, and notice how it feels. Here are some activities where you can become more mindful.

·   Taking a shower

When you are on autopilot you are vaguely aware of how the water feels when you are showering. You battle trying to get the water right, trying to hit that right temp, but then your mind wanders off thinking about what you watched on TV, or what you have to do today. You aren't in the moment.

Instead, start to think about how warm the water is and how it feels as it slides down you. Think of how your shower gel, shampoo, conditioner, or soap smells, and how the bubbles feel on your skin. Once you become used to noticing these things, being more mindful will become easier.

·   Brush your teeth

When you brush your teeth you probably don't think about what you're doing. You've been doing it for years and it's not that hard. You stare at your reflection and focus more on how your skin looks than what you are doing. You may even have to run through your house with the toothbrush sticking out of your mouth.

Instead, start thinking about the texture and taste of the toothpaste and brush. Think of how the brush feels as you move it in your mouth. Think of how the floor feels under feet and your arm feels as it moves. Be mindful as you brush each of your teeth.

·   Drive to work

You slide into your car, bus, or train and you sit there mindlessly staring out the window. Even when you're driving, you don't focus on what is going on around you, you're thinking about what you are going to have to do. The man sitting next to you on the bus feel asleep on your arm and you don't even notice until you have to get off.

Instead, pay attention to the people around you. Whether you drive yourself or take public transportation, look at what's around, how they look and smell. Notice how the ride feels, is it bumpy or smooth? What kind of things do you pass by? Notice little details that you normally would have overlooked.

· Wash dishes

Most people have a dishwasher now, but when you have to wash dishes by hand you moan as you approach the sink because of the menial task. You robotically scrub, rinse, and dry; over, and over again.

Instead, notice how it feels. Feel the water on your hands. Notice how the scrubber feels when you rub it against the dishes. Notice the difference between how the dirty dishes feel and the clean dishes feel.

· Stand in line

There are lots of times where you will find yourself standing in line; the grocery store, shopping mall, DMV, wherever. You stand there, trying not to make eye contact, and groaning about the time that it's taking.

Instead, start looking at things, noticing them. Notice what the area really looks like. Look at the people around you, don't stare, they may take offense to that. Notice the smells, hopefully, they are pleasant. Take advantage of this moment to notice your surrounds, and to become more aware.

Beyond making sure that you notice things about normal tasks you do every day, you can start adding other actions into your life that will, over time, make you more mindful. Here are a few.

1.   Mindfully eat

When you sit and eat without thinking about what you're doing, either by being on your phone or watching TV, you miss the joy of eating. You don't taste how the food tastes. You don't smell the food. It can also keep you from feeling full and satisfied. This is because your mind thinks you have missed out on eating since there weren't any other sensory triggers. Try not to do fifty things while you are eating. When it's time to eat, sit down and focus only on your food, and not everything else.

2.   Mindfully Walk

Walking may just seem like something you have to do to get from place to place, but it's more than that. When you walk, don't just walk, notice how it feels. Notice how your body moves and the things around you. Take note of the way your feet touch the ground and the muscles that it takes for you to pick up your feet. Observe the sounds and sights that are around you as you walk.

3.   Take Note Of Your Breath

Breathing is rhythmical and a natural occurrence. When you take the time to notice it, it will bring your mind to the present and end, for a moment, the wandering thoughts in your head. You are free from your own thoughts for a few minutes. In that moment, as you think about your breath, you have no fears or worries about anything, you are just there.

4.   Please Your Senses

Involve all of your senses; sight, touch, sound, smell, and taste. These give you a way into the moment. When you are only in your head your senses don't get to work for you. You've heard the phrase "stop and smell the roses", well, that's what you need to do. Notice the smell of the coffee you're drinking. Smell the salty air at the beach. See the color and diversity of the flowers around you. Take notice of the smell and taste of the pizza you eat. Feel how your clothes move across your body. Smell and feel the clean sheets on the bed. Feel the warmth and comfort of your significant other's kiss. Notice the feel of grass under your feet. How the water feels when you take a bath or wash your hands. Use all of your senses as you go throughout your day.

5.   Take Pause During The Day

Take a moment and stop what you are doing and just listen to your surroundings. Listen to how the phone sounds like when it rings. Take a moment to notice how your body weight feels in the chair you're sitting in. Take a moment to feel the door handle before you open the door. Taking moments out of your day to pause and ground yourself can make you more aware and mindful. It also gives you a chance to clear your mind and can give you a boost of energy. Picture it as if these pauses are bookends to begin and end tasks throughout your day.

6. Listen With Your Heart

We as humans have a tendency to not actually listen to what people say when they are talking to us. They are either absentmindedly thinking about what they are going to do, or something that just happened to them. They could also be judging what the other person is saying or just lost in a daydream. The next time you are talking to somebody, make sure you actually listen to what they are saying. Don't let yourself get lost in thought. If you notice you are straying from their words, bring yourself back. You don't have to worry about what you are going to say in response because your mind will know what to say, and it's okay to pause for a moment after they finish before you begin.

7. Lose Yourself In What You Love

Each of us has things that we really love doing. They are what help us connect to our spirit and help us feel completely alive. It could be swimming, cooking, building things, dancing, painting, hiking, gardening, singing, or writing. It doesn't matter what it is. When you participate in these activities you'll find that you will lose yourself in them. This doesn't mean you go into autopilot. In these tasks, you lose the part of you that is constantly worrying about things. It quiets your mind because you love doing it and you are solely focused in that present moment. Start doing more of the activities during the week, and your happiness will improve.

8.   Daily Meditation

Meditation has lots of benefits, many of which we have already covered. You will have more energy, inspiration, peace, and happiness. You don't have to have a lot of time to meditate. 10 minutes a day can positively affect your day to day life. This will also boost your mindfulness, so it will become easier to use mindfulness during your day.

9.   Mix Up Your Day To Day

There are lots of reasons why you feel so happy during the holiday season. When you travel to different places your mind will automatically become more mindful. This happens because there are new smells, sights, and sounds to experience. The senses naturally take over and it frees your mind so you can live in the moment. If you don't have time to travel somewhere, that's okay. You can get the same effect by switching up your normal day to day routine. Instead of driving the same way to work every day, change up your route. Try a different coffee shop. Shop in places you have never been in, or participate in some local adventure, or learn something new.

10. Take Notice Of Emotions And Thoughts

You've heard me say this before; you are not your thoughts; you only observe your thoughts. Since you can listen to what your thoughts are, that proves they aren't you. You're separate from your thoughts. Simply acknowledging them and observing them without any judgment allows you to become more present in your life. This keeps you from getting caught up in the constant flow of your thoughts. When you take notice of your thoughts, avoid letting them carry you away. Think of the thought like a train. You're standing on the platform and you just watch as the trains come in and as they leave. You don't try to jump on them and let them take you to some unknown place.

Traits of the Mindful Person

Mindful people are going to live their life differently than the autopilot person. Here are some ways to know if a person is a mindful person.

They take lots of walks.

It's easy in our crazy world to become burnout and exhausted, and the mindful person knows how to solve that problem. Through walking. They know that they can go on a walk to clear their mind and to help them calm their thoughts. A walk can give them more awareness and a new perspective. Also, being in nature and seeing all the greenery might actually be good for the brain and send it to a meditative space. Studies have shown that walking outside gives you the ability for involuntary attention, which means that your mind can focus on the present and you can also have the chance to reflect.

Daily tasks are done mindfully.

Like I mentioned earlier, taking a notice of the little things that happen during your normal tasks is a good way to be mindful. Noticing how things feel, taste, and smell brings you into the moment.

They create things.

Mindfulness can boost your creative ability. Mindful people will naturally start doing more creative things during their day. The act of creative work can help you place your mind in a meditative state. If you are having problems in regular meditation, doing something like drawing, cooking, or singing can help you meditate.

They listen to their breath.

I've covered this a lot. Mindful people notice everything about their breathing. They don't breathe on autopilot.

They don't multitask.

Multitasking will keep people from being able to focus on things that they are doing. It is the enemy of mindfulness. Most people, though, multitask throughout their whole day. Some studies have discovered that when a person's attention is divided between tasks, it will take them 50% longer to finish the task. Errors are also more likely to happen. You need to make sure that you only focus on one thing at a time. Interruptions will happen, but you have to bring yourself back to the one task at hand.

They check their phone at the right time.

People who are mindful keep their relationship with electronics healthy. This could be making sure that as soon as they wake up they don't reach for their phone to check their e-mail. The same goes for bedtime too. They may even go so far as to keep their phone in a completely different room than the one that they sleep in. They may even turn it off on the weekends or on vacation so that they can unplug. The biggie is that they turn off their phones when they are with family and friends. This allows them to mindfully interact with the people around them.

They look for new experiences.

Mindful people are open to new things. People that prioritize peace of mind and presence will enjoy savoring the little moments and big moments in life. Having new experiences will make you more mindful as well.

They venture outside.

Making time to experience the outdoors is a powerful way to reboot your mind and give you a sense of wonder and ease. The outdoors can help you to relieve stress and boost energy and attention. You will find that your memory will become better after you have spent some time outside.

They know what they are feeling.

Contrary to popular belief, mindfulness isn't solely about being happy every moment of the day. Instead, it's about accepting what happens and how you feel. If you are constantly preoccupied with being happy, you are only hurting yourself in the long run. You will constantly focus on the fact that you are not happy, and that only causes you to be unhappy.

They take the time to meditate.

This has been talked about a lot. Meditation plays a large role in being mindful, and mindful people know and understand that.

They know the mind and body.

People tend to shove food in their mouth without thinking about how it tastes, or if it's making them feel full. Mindful people will make sure they notice everything about what they eat and how their body responds to it.

They don't take themselves seriously.

People like to worry about everything they have done and the problems they have. A mindful person doesn't do that. They keep their sense of humor even when there are problems going on in their life.

They allow their mind to wander.

Mindfulness is about being present, but letting your mind wander is also important. Mindful people are able to find that happy medium between mindful and autopilot. If you stay constantly present, you may miss out on connections between your mind and the world. Using your imagination may even help your mindfulness in the long run.

Chapter 11 Guided Meditations

Breathing has a very important place in all kinds of meditations. Breathing helps in building quick focus and prevents diversion of mind. It is a very effective way to calm your mind and bring your focus to one point. This is a part of meditation that you will have to do from the very first day. Rhythmic breathing can play a very important role in quickly dissipating your anger, stress, and anxiety. When you breathe mindfully, you can actually help your body in lowering the blood pressure. It increases the flow of oxygen in the body and reduces the amount of carbon dioxide.

Relaxed Rhythmic Breathing

In this exercise, your complete focus should remain on your inhalations and exhalation.

- Your breathing should remain natural
- Don't try to force your breathing
- Simply become fully aware of every breath you take
- You must try to focus all your attention on the breath you take
- Feel its warmth
- Follow its path through your nostrils

- Initially, you may have distracting thoughts, you don't need to fear
- Simply acknowledge your thoughts and divert your attention back to your breathing
- Follow your inhalations and exhalations
- As you breathe with greater focus, your breathing would become deeper and slower
- Don't try to change anything or force your breathing pattern
- Simply try to find your natural breathing pace
- The more focused breathing you'll have, the calmer you'll get
- This is the best way to go into the meditative state
- Through this method, your mind becomes focused and you have better control over your thoughts and emotions

You can repeat this breathing exercise several times a day. Doing it early in the morning in fresh air is the best. This rhythmic breathing would help you in calming the mind chatter. You'll be more at peace in your mind. It is also a great exercise to relax and relieve stress. If you want to practice the steadiness of the body and mind, then also this breathing exercise is very helpful.

Pranayam or Breathing through Alternate Nostrils

This is one of the most popular breathing exercises advised in yoga. It has tremendous health benefits and it also helps in bringing focus and clarity of mind. This exercise is simple and can be performed in the morning and evening hours.

- Sit in the meditation posture, preferably cross-legged
- You'll need to hold your nostril from one hand, choose your active hand for the same
- Place your other hand in your lap in a resting position
- Keep your back and neck straight
- Now place your thumb on one of the nostrils and close it
- From the other nostril inhale deeply
- Release the nostril covered by your thumb
- Now using your middle finger close the other nostril and exhale fully
- From this nostril itself, inhale deeply
- Cover this nostril now and use the other nostril to exhale and inhale
- This process needs to be repeated several times

This breathing exercise is excellent for your health and also for beginning your meditation sessions.

Controlled Breathing

This breathing exercise is helpful for releasing all the stress and tension from your body. This breathing exercise is used extensively at the beginning of meditation to release the accumulated stress in the body and for bringing the mind to focus.

- Sit in the meditation position
- Inhale deeply
- Take in as much air as you can
- While you inhale, remain mindful of the movement of the air through your nostrils
- Imagine the air to be a ray of light
- Follow the path it takes in your body
- Feel it filling your lungs
- Observe the expansion of your chest as the air fills in it
- Keep inhaling till you feel your gut has got filled with the air
- Now hold your breath for a brief moment
- Simply count till 5
- 1....2....3.....4.....5

- Now exhale slowly through your mouth
- Try to empty out all the air inside your body
- Feel your gut getting empties
- Observe your chest getting deflated
- Repeat the process several times
- While exhaling feel as if this air is going to take away all the stress, tension, negativity, and diseases from your body
- This exhalation should make you feel lighter

This meditation helps in building pinpoint focus on the activity of breathing. All the mental distractions go away as your complete focus is on controlling the breath.

These are simple breathing exercises that can help you a lot in building deep focus and they also help in achieving the meditate state faster.

Cardiac Coherence Exercise

This meditation helps you to get in touch with your heart, to allow you to make choices more and more adherent to your most intimate desires and connect to your spirit.

The first few times you experience it, you may not feel the response of your heart. Continue to persevere and you will soon have results.

Sit comfortably in the place you have chosen to listen to this exercise.

Close your eyes and take a deep breath.

Breathe in and breathe out through the nose at all times.

Now take your natural breath and bring attention to your physical body.

Start relaxing from the head. Relax the muscles of your face, eyes, and mouth.

Relax your neck and shoulders, the arms up to your hands.

Now relax your chest and your belly.

Continue relaxing your back and spine.

Also relax the buttocks and thighs, and the legs down to the feet.

Inhale and exhale slowly, without forcing your breath. Simply listen to the air coming in through your nose and always coming out through your nose.

Very good, just like that.

Take a few more breaths.

If you feel any tension, physical or emotional discomfort, inhale and exhale deeply and let that discomfort simply come out of your body.

Whatever you feel, use your breath to gently lead it outward.

Continuing to breathe, bring attention to the center of your chest and try to tune in to your heartbeat.

If you can't feel it, you can place your hand on your chest and listen for a few moments.

Feel what is happening in the center of your chest and memorize these feelings.

Now bring your mind's attention to an image, situation, event in which you were extremely happy.

Your whole body, your mind and your spirit are pervaded by the joy you experienced on that occasion.

Savor every moment, live it completely.

You have plenty of time to be there again.

Keeping vivid all the sensations you are experiencing, brings attention back to the center of your chest.

What do you feel now, in the middle of your chest? It could be a pleasant warmth, a tingling or a feeling of expansion. Whatever you perceive, memorize it without judging it.

Now bring your left hand very slowly and place it to the center of your chest, than place your right hand above it.

Tune in with your heart and stay listening.

Now that you are in tune with your heart, silently formulate the question you would like to ask.

You could start like this:

"My faithful travelling companion, I ask you with great humility for my maximum benefit and for that of all the people involved, if this thing (specify which thing) is useful at this moment for my evolution and for that of the intire universe. Thank you"

So listen to what's going on inside you.

The answer may manifest itself in various ways depending on your sensitivity.

However, what indicates an affirmative answer, it is usually a feeling of great expansion in the center of the chest and of lightness.

Stay in touch with you for a few more moments.

When you feel the right time has come, with your time, slowly open your eyes.

Meditation of the oak

The meditation of the oak is very useful when you feel the need to be more rooted and slow down the chatter of the mind. Your mind becomes lighter, your breathing calms down and your anxiety and stress move away.

Sit comfortably in the place you have chosen to listen to this exercise.

Close your eyes and take a deep breath.

Breathe in and breathe out through the nose at all times.

Now take your natural breath and bring attention to your physical body.

Start relaxing from the head. Relax the muscles of your face, eyes, and mouth.

Relax your neck and shoulders, the arms up to your hands.

Now relax your chest and your belly.

Continue relaxing your back and spine.

Also relax the buttocks and thighs, and the legs down to the feet.

Inhale and exhale slowly, without forcing your breath. Simply listen to the air coming in through your nose and always coming out through your nose.

Very good, just like that.

Take a few more breaths.

If you feel any tension, physical or emotional discomfort, inhale and exhale deeply and let that discomfort simply come out of your body.

Whatever you feel, use your breath to gently lead it outward.

Breathe slowly, simply observe what happens while you breathe.

Listen to your breath without judgment.

Be present in your breath.

Be your own breath.

Now breathe even more deeply.

Inhale through your nose and imagine that your belly swells like a colored balloon until the maximum of its expansion and then hold your breath for a few seconds.

Then exhale from your nose, imagining the balloon slowly deflates.

Repeat for 3 times always imagining the balloon swelling and deflating.

Now take your natural breath again.

Your body is pleasantly relaxed.

Imagine you see a dirt path in front of you.

Start walking slowly so you can look around.

On the sides of this path you see a multitude of colorful flowers.

They're wonderful! And you can even smell them.

You can hear the chirping of birds, the light rustling of tree branches, the sound of a small waterfall in the distance.

There are only Peace and Harmony.

As you continue to walk, you notice a slight warmth on the skin of your face.

It is the sun's rays that warm you up nicely.

Just a few more steps and you realize that the path is finished and that in front of you there is an immense emerald green lawn.

You continue to advance calmly and you see a huge tree in the middle of the lawn.

Something inside you is pushing you to get closer and closer.

As you get closer, you realize that it's not just any old tree, but that you're standing in front of a wonderful, mighty, centuries-old tree: an oak!

Now that you are at its feet, you realize how big and wrinkled its trunk is and how strong its roots are and how deep they push themselves as if they wanted to reach the center of the earth.

Its branches are full of green leaves and stand out high towards the blue sky as if they wanted to touch it.

With great delicacy, first asking permission from this wonderful being of nature, place your hands on its wrinkled trunk.

Instantly you perceive its most precious qualities: its great strength, endurance and flexibility.

It has managed to overcome countless difficulties during its life: floods, earthquakes, hurricanes, fires. Yet it is still here, well rooted on the ground and reaching out into the sunlight.

I invite you now to embrace the trunk of the oak by placing a cheek and making your whole body adhere to it.

Listen to what is going on inside you as you are merge into this regenerating embrace.

Little by little you begin to perceive a flow of energy that from the trunk of the oak enters you and expands to the center of your chest.

It's not just adding energy to you. The oak is giving you a very special gift. It is giving you its most precious qualities: the stability, strength and perseverance of the trunk and its roots, while from its branches and leaves you receive lightness, abundance and flexibility.

Stay in touch with this powerful energy for a few more moments.

Let the qualities of oak penetrate every cell in your body.

And now, very calmly, loosen this embrace.

Take a few steps back and observe the oak in all its majesty.

Thank it for the gift it gave you, with the promise to treasure it.

Now you can turn your back on the oak tree and retrace your steps as you head towards the flowery path.

Take with you all the feelings and emotions you have experienced.

You can recall this deep feeling of well-being whenever you want, in the days, weeks, months to come.

Now take a few deep breaths and start to getting back in touch with your body.

Slowly start moving your fingers and toes while keeping your eyes closed.

If you feel the need, stretch your arms and legs.

Stay in contact with yourself for a few more moments.

Savour this feeling of deep well-being.

When you feel that the right time has come, with your time, slowly open your eyes.

Conclusion

You are well on your way to achieving the life balance you are looking for and you now have all of the tools that you need to stay open and energized.

As you begin to go through your chakra system pay close attention to your own experience. This book has all of the information that you need to help you heal, but your experience will always be unique to you and your intuition will play a big part in your whole experience. Listen to your body and your energy and let it show you the best way to go through this experience, one day at a time.

Now you know all about the chakra system, how they work, the science behind energy and vibrational frequency, and the opportunity to start your Kundalini awakening journey, sparking your dormant life force and purpose into action as you go through the chakra healing process. You are truly giving yourself a gift by opening this book and this doorway to seeking more than what lies on the surface.

This book has also given you all of the knowledge you need to understand what each chakra represents, its qualities and what physical and emotional aspects are affected through each chakra in the body. Learning about the common ailments and issues that can arise from blockages in your energy can help you see beyond what our medical community can't show us. There is always so much more to it than what you can see on the surface.

You have been given a treasure chest of exercises, yoga poses, meditations and even some secret tips on how to open your kundalini energy and your third eye. All of these practices and tips are geared towards showing you the right path to take to reach an enlightened state of being. All of your opportunities for growth are right inside of you and all you have to do is reach in and start looking through your energetic life-force.

As you move forward, you have further suggestions on how to maintain balance and live a healthy and fulfilling life as a fully charged person. Your energy is asking for you to take action and be your truest, most abundant self. This book offers you all of the tools that you need to get started with your healing journey and your transcendence into your lightest, highest vibrational self. Good luck on the path and always refer to this book and your inner knowing along the way!

If this book has been useful to you and you like it, I suggest you also read these my books

"Chakras Guide"
"Chakras Healing for Beginners"

CPSIA information can be obtained
at www.ICGtesting.com
Printed in the USA
BVHW062059250221
601128BV00015B/1652